MW00941333

Hermann's Ruhe

Karin Harrison

by

Karin Harrison

Copyright © 2011 Karin Harrison
All rights reserved.
ISBN: 1456422189
ISBN-13: 9781456422189

This is a work of fiction. The people, events, and circumstances depicted in this novel are fictitious and the product of the author's imagination and any resemblance of any character to any actual person, whether living or dead, is purely coincidental.

For Ingrid Hearn,

My sister and best friend.

Contents

1 **Nights of Terror** – I

2 **Flight from Hermann's Ruhe** – II

3 **The Poplar Tree** – 33

4 **The Warehouse** – 47

5 **The Painting** – 69

6 **The Colonel** – 89

7 **The Homecoming** – I2I

8 **A Time of Peace** – I35

1

Nights of Terror

Wildenheim, Germany

Spring 1945

Sirens wailed into the night. Helen bolted upright, groped for the matches, and lit the candle stump. She heard the grandfather clock in the hallway strike midnight. She reached for her glasses and yawned. The sirens had blared every night this week. She couldn't remember the last time she'd enjoyed the luxury of a full night's sleep. She jumped out of bed and glanced at her image in the mirror above the dresser. She was approaching her fortieth birthday, but her face, so pale and wan, made her look much older. Dark shadows clung underneath her eyes, and deep lines dug into the skin around her mouth. The navy-blue sweat suit that she slept in, hung loosely on her body. She shrugged and reached for her shoes. She had to move fast.

Helen rushed into her children's bedroom. "Paul, Bessie, wake up!" She gently lifted four-year-old Anne from her bed, and the child began to sob. Helen sighed. "Hush, sweetheart," she said, brushing a kiss across the fuzzy red hair of her youngest daughter. Anne snuggled against her mother, clutching her beloved, well-worn teddy firmly by his ear.

Paul, her eldest child, climbed from the sheets and sat on the edge of the bed. He was tall for his fourteen years and terribly thin. He brushed his tousled hair from his half-closed eyes and stretched his long legs. Across the room, his sister did not stir.

"Paul, make sure Bessie gets up. I'll wake Omi and Opa." Helen hurried out of the room. Anne rested her head against her mother's shoulder and, with her thumb in her mouth, drifted off to sleep.

Paul rose and padded across the room. "Wake up." He tugged on the bulky down comforter, which Bessie had pulled over her head. When she didn't move, he yanked it off the bed.

"Leave me alone." She buried her dark head beneath the pillow. She was nine years old and disliked being bullied by her brother. Since her father had been away at war, Paul seemed to have taken on an unprecedented authority, which she resented. She had noticed that her mother often consulted with him. He was allowed to stay up later than his sisters, a rule she often challenged. Five years' difference in age between them was such a trivial thing, and she firmly believed that she should be treated equally.

Helen and her family occupied the first floor of the three-story apartment complex along with her parents, who had lost their home during the very first air strike. Their house had stood on Bahnhofstrasse opposite the railroad station, an area that suffered some of the greatest losses in the city. The bombs hit their targets with precision and annihilated the entire district. The ensuing inferno lasted for days. Only rubble and ruins remained where once stood buildings of magnificent architectural design, dating back over a hundred years.

The beautiful Wildenheim Castle was an eerie shell of scorched sandstone. The staggered remains of the four towers rose from the ruins, lamenting its demise. The gardens bordering the perimeter, once a colorful artwork of diverse flora, had been overrun by a variety of proliferating weeds and brush. Two gaping craters had swallowed some of the huge, gnarled oaks, planted two hundred years earlier by order of the king.

The bombings continued, night after night, inflicting deadly destruction that wiped out nearly 80 percent of the city. The loss of their home with all their possessions had had a profound effect on Helen's father. Hermann had become defiant and stubborn, whereas Rosa, his wife, dealt with the situation in a more realistic manner. They had been through this before. Hermann had fought in France during World War I, where, during a scouting mission, he had stepped on a land mine. He spent many weeks in the field hospital. Despite the primitive conditions, the surgeon managed to save his foot, but the injury left him with a permanent limp. Rosa guided her husband with unwavering firmness and support through the difficult recovery period.

She was unsuccessful, however, in getting him to join the Nazi Party, and, as a result, he became the subject of harassment by the Gestapo, who often hauled him to headquarters. They mocked and threatened him, and when these tactics failed, they resorted to torture. On one occasion, they forced Hermann to stand up naked for hours in a cold room. His lame foot sent spasms of pain up his leg. When he collapsed, they revived him, and the torture continued until he was no longer able to stand up. They could not break him. He despised their party and everything it stood for and suffered their outrage with stoic resignation. Eventually, they decided that he was a harmless old man and left him alone.

Helen walked toward the living room, which served as a bedroom for her parents. She knocked on the door. Dressed in a sweater and wrinkled wool skirt, Rosa stuck her head through the doorway.

"He refuses to get out of bed," she said. They had been sleeping in their clothes for months, ever since the night attacks had begun. It saved time and frustration and got them to the shelter more quickly.

"Do you want me to talk to Dad?" Helen asked.

"He says he's tired of everything and doesn't care anymore. Let the house fall on him," Rosa whispered. "You go ahead and take care of the children. I'll handle him."

Helen gave her mother a reassuring squeeze and headed for the large hallway closet. She snatched the canvas bag containing candles, matches, and blankets and followed Paul, who was walking toward the apartment door, dragging the tired Elisabeth behind him. Rosa and Hermann tagged along. Helen glanced at her father, and he stared at her defiantly. His expression softened when his eyes fell on Anne. He reached for her and gathered her into his arms. Anne whimpered softly and pressed her sleepy face against his, oblivious to the emerging stubble on his cheeks.

The family hurried down the steps toward the rear of the basement, where the air-raid shelter was located. Helen and her family were always the last to arrive. The other tenants were sitting on wooden benches, their faces tense and grim. Helen nodded to the Stringers, who lived on the third floor with their daughter-in-law Mary. The owners of the property, Mr. and Mrs. Brenner, occupied the second floor. They had arrived a few minutes before Helen. Mrs. Brenner sat with her head bowed in devout prayer, her arthritic hands clutching her rosary. She was a big woman with small eyes that glinted malevolently from beneath lowered lids as her ample bosom heaved in rhythmic succession. A huge mole on her chin sprouted dark fuzz. Her husband, a ruddy, stout man, sat next to her, his face stony and eyes fixed upon the tattered Bible resting on his lap.

The nights in the shelter were long and arduous. The room, no larger than twelve by twelve, was small and stifling. Constructed of concrete reinforced by steel, the shelter would provide minimum protection if the building was hit. Plain wooden benches lined the damp walls, and four metal chairs crowded around a small table in the center of the room. The tenants had brought their own candles and had placed them on the table. There had been no electricity for months.

Mrs. Brenner scowled when the first-floor tenants made their appearance. She mumbled under her breath. The Brenners were childless and had zero tolerance for children. Helen's kids were the cause of continued annoyance, and Mrs. Brenner missed no opportunity to express her displeasure. The landlords had imposed strict rules upon their tenants. Each family was allotted a small section of the garden to grow vegetables and flowers; however, the children were banned from that area, or anywhere else on the surrounding property. Mrs. Brenner's kitchen window allowed a clear view of the backyard, and she watched routinely in hopes of catching the unsuspecting villains in any wrongdoing. The kids were always in trouble, and Helen had to summon all her diplomatic skills to appease the complaining landlords.

Mary Stringer jumped up and hurried toward Helen to lend a hand. Short and skinny, Mary was an optimist by nature, which showed in her laughing eyes and dimpled cheeks. She had been married only six months when her husband was called to fight. Helen and Mary had a common bond; their husbands were missing in action, and they'd had no communication in over a year. The two women had become close friends as they commiserated with each other over their fate. Helen was convinced that she would have gone mad without Mary's support during the long hours in the shelter.

"She's been agitated since we got here," Mary whispered casting a furtive glance at Mrs. Brenner.

"I'd give anything not to have to come down here," Helen muttered. "There are times when I am tempted to punch her ugly face."

Mary suppressed a giggle and resumed her seat next to her in-laws.

Anne's muffled sobs had escalated into ear-piercing screams, and they discovered that her beloved teddy was missing. Paul offered to look for him in the stairway, but Mr. Brenner had already locked the heavy steel door. Hermann rocked Anne gently in his arms, but to no avail. She began to scream and then decided to hold her breath. Hermann quickly handed her over to Helen. Mrs. Brenner glowered disapprovingly and pointed an arthritic finger at Helen. "You'd better shut her up. I'm getting a sick headache," she whined.

"A headache should be the least of your worries," Hermann said.

Mrs. Brenner rolled her eyes and shifted her bulk on the bench. She rattled her rosary beads, shooting disapproving glances at her frightened tenants.

Helen paced the small room, rocking Anne in her arms. It was eleven steps one way; she had counted hundreds of times. She observed the people lining the walls, resigned to meeting their fate.

There was a time when their lives were filled with laughter. Helen closed her eyes to the poignant memories that haunted her mind. She could almost smell the fragrant breeze that swept across the river that Sunday afternoon as she sat close to Fritz in the small boat. High up on the cliff, Wildenheim Castle rose proudly, a sentinel, a historical landmark, whose pinnacles of towers, spires, and turrets could be seen for miles. For centuries, it was home to the royal family of the king, who ruled the state quite often with more vigor than wisdom.

They had finished their sandwiches, and the children were enjoying the last of the small dessert cakes. The boat drifted aimlessly. Paul and Bessie had cast their fishing lines and were waiting patiently. Helen turned to her husband and drew his face close to hers. His eyes, an incredible, indefinable shade of hazel, searched hers.

"What is it?" he asked. "You're acting mysteriously today."

"I'm very happy." She paused. "I wonder if it'll be a boy or a girl."

He gave a lurch, causing the small boat to rock precariously.

"Dad, stop it. You're chasing the fish away!" Paul shouted over his shoulder.

"Darling, is it true?" Fritz pulled her close to him.

"Yes. I'm afraid you'll have another mouth to feed. I just found out yesterday. We'll have our baby in May," Helen whispered. "Shall we tell the kids?"

Later on that afternoon, they strolled in the beautiful gardens of Wildenheim Castle and watched the spectacular sunset from the terrace.

Anne sighed in her sleep. Helen kissed her softly on the cheek. What was to become of them? The children deserved a chance at a life free of fear and hunger. Every day, she struggled to provide them with the barest necessities. She worried that the nights in the shelter would inflict lasting emotional damage, although Rosa had assured her that the children would be fine, and told her to quit worrying.

Helen glanced around the room. Everyone was silent, even Mrs. Brenner. Bessie had cuddled up next to her grandfather and gone back to sleep. Helen smiled at her oldest daughter. Bessie had inherited Fritz's dark hair and strong, square chin, and, like Fritz, Bessie was able to fall asleep in any position at any given time; sometimes, she nodded off at the dinner table and had to be carried to her bed.

Helen caught Hermann's eye, and he nodded reassuringly. Like Bessie, she felt a powerful urge to crawl onto his lap, as she used to when she was a child, and the world was crowding in on her. He always managed to make her feel better. Helen blinked, and her eyes welled. Then he winked at her, and she gave him a bittersweet smile. She knew what he was thinking—*One day at a time, one day at a time.* She sat down next to Mary.

The faint drone of airplane engines penetrated the thick walls with increasing velocity. They held their breath. High-pitched whistling melted into a succession of violent blasts that rattled the building. The earsplitting sound of an explosion filled the shelter, and chunks of plaster fell on the terrified group. Mrs. Brenner screamed, "We're hit! We're going to die!" She covered her face.

The Stringers held on to each other; their faces frozen in terror. Hermann put one arm around Rosa and tightened the other arm around the sleeping Elisabeth. Anne woke up and clung to her mother, sobbing quietly. Helen glanced at Paul. He shivered and she pulled him to her. "I am afraid," he said through gritted teeth.

"So am I. It's nothing to be ashamed of," she whispered and closed her eyes as her lips moved in silent prayer. *Please don't make my children suffer. If we are to die tonight, let it be quick.*

Helen focused her gaze straight ahead, wondering if Fritz was still alive. Just last week, she had spoken with her best friend Inge, who showed her a letter from her husband, Werner, dated over a year ago, which had finally arrived. There was no return address.

They couldn't begin to guess where their husbands were fighting the enemy.

Only two days later, a bomb leveled Inge's house and buried everyone beneath a mountain of rubble. The explosion reverberated through the neighborhood and took out most of the remaining windows in the houses nearby. When the sirens signaled that it was safe to leave the air shelters, the neighbors discovered the horrible sight. They worked all day to free the people buried beneath the rubble. Everyone pitched in; even the children helped clear away debris. By late afternoon, they heard someone banging on a pipe. It was a sign of life, but they lacked the tools to speed up the rescue, and by the time they dug through, the only survivor was Ben, Inge's German shepherd.

A familiar sound roused Helen. She opened her eyes. Here it was again: the chime sequence of the grandfather clock in their apartment announcing the fifth hour. Five simple chimes suddenly were the most beautiful sound in the world.

Paul craned his head. He jumped up. "The planes are gone!" he cried.

Everyone strained to hear. Mr. Stringer let out a sharp breath and said, "We made it through another night." The cold room came alive with chatter. There would be other nights like this, but that thought was pushed aside as they reveled in being alive.

Within the next hour, the sirens signaled that it was safe to leave the shelter. Mr. Brenner unlocked the door, and they filed out of their nightly prison, one by one, with Mr. Stringer leading the way. With bated breath, they crept up the stairs. No obstacles blocked their way. The house seemed to be intact. Helen followed her parents, carrying Anne in her arms; Paul and Elisabeth were right behind her. She heard Rosa gasp.

"What is it?" Helen stepped up next to Rosa. The gardens in the back yard had been replaced by a huge crater. Tree limbs and top soil littered the property. A cloud of dust hovered over the chaos of mangled wire fencing and uprooted fruit trees, and black smoke rose from the smoldering embers that used to be the shed.

The group stared in silence.

"Wow, were we lucky!" Paul said, and everyone began to speak at once. They laughed and hugged each other in a sudden euphoria that included even the Brenners.

Rosa took a few steps forward. Her eyes traveled across the jumble that used to be their source of food. "Our precious crop… gone. How much more are we supposed to take? What have we done that we must be punished like this?" Rosa's voice was husky with tears. "What are we going to do now?"

Mr. Stringer held out his hands and said, "We'll clean up and plant anew; that's what we'll do. We'll start a community garden where the shed used to be. There's enough room. It looks like Helen's peach tree survived, and the apple and pear trees in the Brenners' section by the rear fence have been spared. We'll work together and share, equally." He stared boldly at the Brenners, who nodded reluctantly.

"Mutti, look." Bessie pointed to the horizon. The eastern sky rippled a palette of colors, beautiful variations of reds, purples, oranges, and peaches as the sun, dutiful and sure, nudged away the gloom of that awful night. Helen watched the widening bands of gold that embraced the town and lit the hollow towers of Wilden-heim Castle in a celebration of rebirth and renewal that filled their hearts with hope. They were alive. A new day was born.

2

Flight from Hermann's Ruhe

"**W**e've got to get out of here. Now." Hermann limped into the living room.

Helen stared at her father with fear in her eyes. The book of Grimm's fairy tales that she had been reading to Anne dropped to the floor and slammed shut. She rose quickly. "But why, Dad... why?"

Rosa put down her knitting and took off her glasses. She studied her husband's face with a wrinkled brow. He was clearly upset.

"The American troops are camped at our doorstep. Wildenheim will be besieged by air and from the ground." Hermann stared at the pale faces of his family. "This will be the last battle fought over our town, and we're going to go down." He spoke with such conviction it made the prediction unarguable, but Helen tried.

"I heard yesterday that we have enough firepower to fight back—"

Hermann interrupted her impatiently, "I don't know why we're being told these lies. Germany should have surrendered long ago; it would have saved lives and property. With that madman in charge, we never had a chance. We must concentrate on our survival. We've made it this far, and we're not going to die now."

Helen trembled. Her knees felt weak. What next? When will it end? Just when they had determined that things could not get any worse, they were confronted with another problem.

"We're going up to Hermann's Ruhe. It's our only chance. Pack only what we can carry...and hurry," Hermann said.

Helen rushed out of the room. Anne began to cry. "I'm scared, Omi..."

Rosa picked her up. "No reason to be scared, sweetheart. You always have fun at the cottage. We'll play games—"

"Rosa, get going. We don't have time to waste," Hermann urged. "Where's Paul?"

"He's playing soccer at Bauer's field. Bessie went with him. I'll go get them." Rosa placed Anne on the floor and took her hand. "Come, sweetheart; you'll go with me."

Less than an hour later, the old wooden cart had been stacked with only the most essential of their belongings. The children wore backpacks stuffed with clothing; Anne hugged her beloved teddy. He had recently lost an eye; the remaining eye stared impassively at Mary Stringer who met them at the gate.

"Have you heard?"

"What now?" Hermann frowned.

"They're urging all the women and children to leave town by noon today, at which time, a curfew will be in effect and no one will be allowed to leave their house, much less the town."

"Looks like were leaving not one minute too soon," Helen said. "What're you going to do?"

"I don't want to stay here and spend the entire time in the air shelter with the Brenners. We'll head out to Leiderbach and stay with my sister," Mary said.

"You'd better hurry." Helen gave Mary a quick hug. "Good luck. May God be with you."

"May God be with us all." Mary ran up the steps.

The ten-mile trip to Hermann's Ruhe had never seemed as long as it did that day. Perched up on the hill, the small hunting lodge sat in the middle of open fields that bordered the dense forest of the Spessart. Hermann and Franz, Fritz's father, had laid the foundation in 1933. Paul was only four years old at the time. By the summer of 1934, they were able to bring in furniture, just when Helen found out that she was expecting Bessie. Fritz had insisted on the construction of a small concrete pool for his son and the new baby on the way. Water was no problem at the time, since the well brought forth lots of it. Paul loved to spend time in the pool trying to catch little green frogs. The cottage became the site of many happy gatherings with family and friends. Now its isolated location could save their lives.

The cart creaked and fussed as Paul and Helen labored to pull it across the gravelly road. "I'm tired," Anne complained and looked longingly at the old baby carriage pushed by Bessie. It was stacked with blankets and the last few jars of preserved food prepared by Rosa the year before.

"We're almost there, sweetheart," Helen said.

Rosa sighed deeply; they hadn't even covered half the distance. She picked up Anne. "I'll carry you...but only for a little while." She turned and cast a worried glance at Hermann who followed some distance behind; his limp slowed him down, and she knew he was in pain.

"Let's take the shortcut." Paul pointed to the path that branched off to their right; steep and rocky, it led into the woods.

"We'll never be able to pull the old cart up that hill. It's too heavy." Helen turned to Rosa. "Mother, put Anne down," she said. "Make her walk."

When Rosa complied, Anne began to scream. She dropped to the ground and refused to budge. "Just drag her along!" Helen exclaimed, her voice rising shrilly.

"Let's see." Paul fussed with the stacked cart. "If we get rid of the cage and trap, we'll have some room for her."

"Very well. Take it up the embankment and hide it beneath the brush. We can retrieve it later," Helen said.

"No, don't do that…" Herman had caught up with them.

"Dad, we have no choice. It's too far to carry Anne the rest of the way."

"What'll we do for food?" Hermann protested.

"I don't know. We'll worry about that later. Let's move on. I want to reach the cottage before dark." Helen fought to control her growing exasperation.

They arrived at the crossing and turned right to follow the narrow, winding dirt road. Helen glanced at the restaurant to her left. The Spessart Hof looked deserted. How many happy hours they had spent there! She smiled wistfully when she passed the location of their mishap so long ago. After an excellent dinner and far too much wine in the company of their friends Bertl and Karl, they bid farewell to Hans, the owner of the Spessart Hof. He cautioned them to drive carefully, but they laughed and told him not to worry. They got into the old Mercedes and sped up the hill. Fritz swerved to avoid a deer, and the car landed in a ditch. After they had checked their limbs and realized that no one was hurt, they surveyed the damage. They needed help to free the car and decided to walk the rest of the way. Karl entertained them with anecdotes from his youth, which he delivered with detailed animation; the echo of their laughter lingered in the night.

It was the laughter she missed most; there hadn't been much of it lately. Helen's hands tightened around the handle of the cart. Perspiration trickled down her face. What was to become of them? Would the children grow up remembering this nightmare? Would it jade their future—if there was to be a future at all? She turned to check on Anne, who slept peacefully on top of the bumpy cart. She lay nestled against the two large milk cans filled with water. Helen smiled when she heard Rosa explain to Bessie the different ways the varied vegetation growing abundantly in the woods could be used to create a meal. Bessie was taking a great interest in cooking and often hung around the kitchen to watch Rosa.

They turned the corner and carefully navigated the rocky footpath leading to the front gate. The climbing rosebush had taken over the iron trellis arching the gate. The delicate fragrance invaded their senses. Hermann unlocked the gate with the large key, and they padded down the gravelly path leading through the orchard to the little white house.

"Hermann's Ruhe," the wooden plaque carved by Fritz welcomed them from beneath the eaves. Hermann's Ruhe meant Hermann's quietude, a place of tranquility. The green shutters contrasted with the white stucco walls. Red gingham curtains, made by Rosa, were visible through the kitchen window facing the front gate. The roof extended across the front porch that stretched along the entire length of the cottage. Two columns at each end of the porch supported the roof and framed the stone railings. Several rustic wooden chairs and a small table had been turned around and rested against the wall.

Helen removed Anne from the cart and carried her up the porch steps. The view was breathtaking. The rolling hills stretched as far as she could see. The sky was like soft blue silk as it yielded to the golden warmth of the setting sun. Patches of clouds floated across the ridge and into the valley below, where the Main River hugged the town and hurried on as Wildenheim lingered in deceptive peace and tranquility. An owl hooted from the towering Scotch pines in the backyard. A buzzard circled high above. Helen looked up; tears ran down her face.

"It's hard to believe how much destruction and chaos exist down there." Hermann stood next to her. He inhaled deeply. "Coming here is like stepping back into another world, where peace and tranquility surround me, but then this has always been my favorite place."

"I know, Dad." Helen leaned her head against his shoulder. "We have so many happy memories and must be grateful, because those days are gone forever."

"Let's get the stuff unloaded." Rosa bustled past them and stepped into the kitchen. "I'm starved. Paul, fetch some water," she said.

"That wife of mine never wastes time on sentimentalities. She's always been a practical woman." Hermann chuckled in appreciation of his own wit. He entered the house, walked into the small living room, and opened the windows. An oak table and a corner bench placed beneath the four windows facing the porch and the side of the cottage served as a dining area. The bench was covered with comfortable cushions that matched the floral-print curtains. The large oak table was the result of a team effort by Franz, Fritz, and Hermann, and they had proudly carved their initials beneath the table leaf.

A corner hutch with glass doors revealed a set of beer steins with pewter lids and a variety of colorful, hand-painted ceramic bowls that were displayed at Rosa's insistence, since they were far too pretty to hide in the kitchen cabinet. Hermann walked over to the small sofa. Its rich mustard color reflected in the yellow, orange, and pale green pattern Rosa chose when she crocheted the afghan draped across the back. Crewel-stitched cushions made by Rosa and Helen depicted the local wildlife and a sampling of the beautiful native wildflowers. The shelf above the sofa held some of Hermann's beloved leather-bound books. He pulled out a volume and handled it carefully as he glanced through it.

"So…you're going to read a book now, when we've got lots of work to do?" Rosa peered around the doorframe. She smiled softly and without waiting for an answer went on about her business. Hermann replaced the book and proceeded toward the two bedrooms in the rear of the house. The beds made up most of the furnishings in the medium-size rooms, with two double beds in one bedroom and two double beds and Helen's old crib in the other. He fluffed the down comforters and opened the windows to allow the breeze to move freely through the cottage.

The night was deep blue; the stars felt close enough to touch.

"What I wouldn't give for a good cigar." Hermann had joined Helen on the porch.

"Did you get kicked out of the kitchen too?" Helen asked with a smile. Rosa had taken over in a fuss of competence and chased them away. They had eaten their meager dinner, which the children had gulped down. Bessie and Anne were already asleep, and Paul had stretched out on the living room couch to read a book.

"Tomorrow morning, we've got to go down to the stream and fetch water." Rosa stood in the doorway. The cottage had no plumbing, and the well had run dry long ago. Two huge water barrels placed beneath the rainspouts provided one source of water, but they depended on the stream about a half mile down the hill.

"Mutti…" Anne appeared in the doorway rubbing her eyes. "Got to go potty."

"Come, sweetheart." Helen took her hand and led her down the porch steps where the bathroom adjoined the rear of the house. A pitcher of water and a medium-size bowl sat on a wooden stand; a linen towel draped from a hook attached to the wall. A long-legged spider had made its home on top of the round wicker mirror, where intricately woven webs functioned as deadly traps. The bathroom was little more than an outhouse, and Anne hated it. All kinds of creepy bugs scattered whenever she entered. She clung to her mother, who lit the candle on the shelf beneath the mirror. It spread eerie shadows across the whitewashed walls. Anne hesitated, but her mother nodded reassuringly, and she sat down on the toilet. One hand firmly clasping her mother's, she nervously eyed the moving silhouettes on the ceiling.

It sounded like fireworks at first but escalated into recurring blasts amid the roar of airplane engines. Hermann pushed the chessboard aside, and rushed outside. Anne followed. Hundreds of airplanes littered the sky, dropping their bombs on the town below. Fire and smoke proclaimed the annihilation of lives and property.

Anne stood at Hermann's side and latched onto his arm. Rosa deserted the rock garden and hurried up the steps. They stared at the horrifying spectacle.

"This is the end," Rosa said as she wiped her eyes.

"I've rarely seen them attack during the day with such ferocity," Hermann said.

"Where are Helen and the kids?" Rosa fretted.

"Don't worry; they'll be okay." Hermann put his arm around Rosa. "It's a long haul up the hill with those heavy water cans. I think I hear the rickety cart now."

Helen and Paul appeared through the gate pulling the heavy cart, as Bessie pushed from the rear.

"Dad, what's happening?" Helen shouted.

"This is the final battle." Hermann twisted his face into a painful grimace.

Helen shivered. She thought of her friends and neighbors who had decided to stay in town. She prayed that Mary and her family made it out in time. Her eyes swept across the green meadow beneath the orchard and the flowering shrubs that had thrived there for more than a decade. The rock garden had exploded into a burst of color under Rosa's diligent attention. Hermann's Ruhe was their refuge, and she was grateful to have a place where her family was safe.

"Look at those fireworks," Paul said as he watched in awe.

"There are people dying down there as we speak, Paul," Hermann said softly. "It could have been us." He paused. "We don't know how long we can stay here. The worst is yet to come."

Helen stared at her father and froze. Where would they go? Her heart pounded, and the sound of roaring blood filled her ears. She reached out, and they came together and joined hands. They stood for a long time with their heads bowed, and they prayed. They prayed for the people in the battered town and for Fritz, whose whereabouts were unknown. They prayed for courage to sustain them through the dangerous times ahead, and they thanked God for being alive. They stood, huddled together, as the brilliant fireworks created a deadly inferno that swallowed up the town below.

The battle went on day and night for eight long days. Palls of smoke wrapped around Wildenheim like a dirty blanket. Helen paced the front porch, stopping only when there was a break in the barrage. She strained to hear, hoping against hope, but the attack resumed. She stared at the clear, blue sky above the cottage.

"I can't stand it any longer." She covered her ears.

"I wish I knew exactly what the status is down there," Hermann said. "How long can they resist? I think I'm going to head down to the main road and see what I can find out." He took his cane, its silver handle slightly tarnished, and turned to leave, but Helen stopped him.

"I'll go with you."

"No. You stay here." He limped down the steps. "Tell Rosa I went for a walk," he said over his shoulder.

Helen watched him shuffle down the path and through the gate. He chose the long way, turned right, and disappeared from view. *If only we had our bicycles,* she thought. They always brought them up to Hermann's Ruhe. They had been stored in the shed in the backyard in town before the bomb strike, which left a hole deep enough to collect a substantial amount of water. The children called it their pond. It attracted brown mottled toads, which on occasion found their way into the bathtub.

Helen stepped off the porch. Rosa was on her hands and knees. The weeds in the rock garden didn't stand a chance against Rosa's vigorous attack. Dirt flew all about her. The rock garden was Rosa's pride and joy, and the focus of much admiration by their friends.

"What's Herman up to? I saw him leave." Rosa sat back on her heels and wiped her brow. Tiny twigs and leaves had lodged in her hair. Smudges of dirt on her forehead and cheeks made her look like one of the Gypsies who lived in the cave down by the stream. Helen suppressed a smile.

"He's going for a walk," she said.

"You should have given him a basket; he could have picked some blueberries along the way."

"Blueberries are the last thing on his mind." Helen fell on her knees, and, together, they worked in silence.

"That's it for today. I'm exhausted," Rosa said. Helen gathered the discarded weeds and dropped them in a crate.

"I'll take these up to the compost heap." She lifted the crate and paused when she noticed the stillness. She dropped the container and ran up the porch steps. The town was cloaked in black smoke. She looked up; the sky was clear, and the airplanes were gone.

"What's happening?" Rosa had joined her.

Helen shook her head. "I guess that's it."

"It could be temporary," Rosa suggested, when the dry crunch of footsteps drew her attention to the gate. "Here comes Hermann now. Maybe he knows something."

He hurried toward them as fast as his crippled leg would allow. Helen noticed his worried face, and chills crept up her spine. He stumbled up the porch steps and dropped into a chair. He was panting and limp with fatigue. Helen ran into the kitchen and got some water. "Here, Dad. Drink it slowly. Take your time; then tell us what happened." They waited anxiously for him to speak.

"Wildenheim has surrendered. The Americans are in charge," Hermann said. His breath came in short puffs. He took another sip of water. "I ran into Hans at the Spessart Hof," he said. "He showed me a flyer refugees from town had given him. These flyers were dropped all over Wildenheim and explain the details of the surrender." Beads of perspiration trickled down his face. Hermann pulled out his handkerchief and wiped them away. "Hans and his family had already fled to Wasserdorf. He had returned to retrieve some provisions. We must go there right away." Hermann paused. "The lucky guy still had his bike..."

"But why, if the war is over, aren't we safe right here?" Rosa interrupted.

"No. The Americans have pulled all the foreign workers from the region and housed them in the surviving military barracks on Glenheim Strasse. The curfew still exists; however, it doesn't apply to the foreign workers. They're looting and burning what's left standing in town, beating up people, and raping our women. They will show up here in no time, rest assured."

Helen's heart skipped a beat. Her hand flew to her mouth.

"Don't forget that they were brought here against their will, to work in the factories while our men are at war. They had to leave their families behind to fend for themselves. There are thousands of them in Wildenheim; most of them don't speak German. They've suffered oppression and abuse just like us. Their wages barely covered subsistence. They've reason to be angry and now have an opportunity to settle the score."

"We had nothing to do with their demise," Rosa protested.

"You must remember, we're victims, just like these guys, except we've had a choice. We were fools to trust a madman and put him in charge." Hermann rose from the chair. "We can't waste any more time. We must leave immediately. Call the children."

Rosa ran into the living room and hurriedly stuffed sweaters and blankets into a large tote. Helen called the children, who had been playing checkers in the gazebo.

"What's up?" Paul stared at the three terrified adults.

"Let's go." Hermann took Anne's hand, and he led the way.

"Wait! I've got to lock up!" Rosa shouted.

He turned and said calmly, "Don't bother; they'll only break down the door. Leave it wide open."

Rosa stared speechlessly at her husband's back.

"Come along, Mother." Helen hooked her hand through Rosa's arm and led her down the steps. The children had already caught up with Hermann. They passed through the gate and turned left, heading for the woods.

Helen and Rosa ran down the path. Helen glanced briefly at the little house surrounded by trees, flowering shrubs, and an impeccable rock garden. The pines in the backyard yielded their branches and bade them *Godspeed*.

"Why doesn't he wait for us?" Rosa complained. "We're going to lose them in the forest."

A gunshot echoed in the woods, and Rosa's tote was ripped from her hand. She gasped. Another bullet whizzed past her and spat itself out in the forest. They heard snatches of voices from the hill above them. They ran until they reached the safety of the woods where they found Hermann leaning against the robust trunk of a white pine. His breath came in heavy gulps. Anne sobbed between hiccups and reached for her mother. Paul and Bessie had dropped onto the soft carpet of pine needles.

They felt the tremors of pounding footsteps drawing near, and the frightened family hustled forward.

"We must take cover behind the trees; the brush will help conceal us." Hermann yanked his head sideways as a bullet lodged in the tree next to him; pieces of bark hit his face. They ran, keeping low. Prickly branches struck at their faces and arms. They had covered less than a mile when Hermann collapsed on the ground. Rosa tried to pull him up. "It's no use," he said. "You guys go on. I'll take my chances hiding in the bushes."

"We're not leaving you," Rosa said firmly.

"Lean on me, Opa." Paul tried to pull him up.

"Wait." Helen listened. "I don't hear them anymore. Maybe they've given up."

They trudged on, their footsteps inaudible. The stillness was profound. *Even the birds are silent,* Helen thought. They reached the main road, bypassed the Spessart Hof restaurant, and headed toward Wasserdorf.

"Dad, what makes you think we'll be safe in Wasserdorf?" Helen whispered.

"According to Hans, the town folks have barricaded themselves in the schoolhouse. There's safety in numbers," Hermann said. "It's our only chance."

They arrived at the tiny town of Wasserdorf, nestled by the Weisswasser stream, flowing undisturbed as it had for centuries through the vast farmland that stretched throughout the valley. Miraculously, Wasserdorf had suffered very little damage, and most buildings were intact. The streets were deserted. When they came to the schoolhouse, they noticed the boarded-up windows.

Exhausted, they sat on the rough stone boundary surrounding the building. Helen and Paul climbed the broad steps, and she knocked on the door. There was no answer. She could hear voices inside. What if they refused to take them in? She raised her fist and banged on the massive door. Finally, a voice yelled, "We have no more space."

"Please let us in. We won't take up much room," Helen cried. Silence radiated from behind the door.

"You can't leave us out here. Take my children. Surely you have room for three children," she pleaded. "Don't let my children die." Her voice had escalated into a scream. She kicked at the door until her bloody toes poked through the worn shoes. Oblivious to the pain, she sobbed. "We've been hunted, shot at..." Her head slumped against the splintery wood as tears streamed down her face.

"Let them in," a voice thundered. The massive door squealed open, and a woman appeared. Her snow-white hair hung straight to her shoulders, but her face was smooth and her eyes bright. Helen guessed that they were the same age. The woman pulled Helen inside and motioned for the rest of the family to enter. The door slammed shut behind them, and two women dropped a large wooden bolt into place. When her eyes had adjusted to the darkness, Helen realized that they stood in a small foyer. A flight of steps led up to the classrooms. People sitting on blankets took up all the floor space. Some had stretched out and were sleeping.

"I'm Wilma." The woman extended her hand. "Follow me. Be careful. Don't step on anyone."

Helen picked up Anne, and they carefully placed one foot in front of the other. They climbed the stairs, and Wilma pointed to the wall. "This way." A young woman stood, rocking a baby; her eyes stared blankly ahead. "This is my daughter." Wilma fussed with two blankets and spread them out, as the people around them made room for Helen and her family. *Squished like sardines in a can,* Helen thought and smiled gratefully as she turned to Wilma. "Thank you so much for sharing your space with us."

"You're lucky to have escaped those murderous thieves. I've heard that the foreign workers have taken over Wildenheim and the Americans aren't doing a thing about it. We're fairly safe in here." Wilma pointed to the front door where two women and a teenage boy stood guard, an ax and several large clubs at their side. The boy clutched a meat cleaver. "We take turns guarding the door. If they show up here, we'll be ready for them," Wilma said.

Helen shuddered. "We'll take our turn. My son is strong, and so am I," she said.

"We're going to survive." Wilma patted her arm reassuringly. "All we've left is our lives, and we'll fight like the devil to keep them."

Helen was not convinced but nodded as she contemplated the weary group around her.

They spent seven days inside the schoolhouse. Helen marveled at the courtesy the people extended to each other. There were two women teachers who separated the children into age groups and gave lessons each day. The adults gathered and told stories, the only requirement being that they must be happy ones. Three times a day, a scout went outside through a back window to check out the area, and once he declared it safe, the front door was opened to allow everyone a brief outing. Fifteen minutes in the warm sun was barely enough to charge their resources, but the seed of hope had sprung inside them and brought with it the promise of a future.

After the seventh day, early in the morning, the church bell rang. Rosa nudged Hermann. "Listen. I've never heard a more beautiful sound."

The whole building came alive. They opened the front door, and the people streamed outside into the hammering rain. They got soaked, but no one cared. They stretched their limbs and deeply inhaled the fresh air.

White flyers littered the ground. Helen picked one up and read it. She turned to her parents. "It's over...at last," she said. "It says here that the Americans have taken control. They're sending the foreign workers back to their own countries. The looting and killing has stopped."

Wilma walked up to Helen. "We can all go home now...if there's anything left of our homes, that is."

"We have our lives, and that's all that matters...and we've made new friends." Helen clung to Wilma. During the seven days in the schoolhouse, the two women had forged a bond that would last a lifetime.

The family gathered and began the trek up the hill. Blustery squalls of rain pounded their backs. They crossed the little stream, which hurried along, swollen with muddy water. They shivered in their wet clothes as they left the safety of the forest and cautiously stepped into the clearing. The path leading to the front gate of Hermann's Ruhe was deserted. The downpour had created deep rivulets that carried small rocks and soil down the hill, making the uphill climb a tricky affair. They arrived at the gate; it stood wide open. The jasmine growing along the fence was in full bloom; the flowered branches reached out to them.

They approached the cottage, and Rosa cried out. Torn, dirty clothes were scattered on the ground. The rain barrels were gone. The beautiful wooden chairs on the porch were reduced to kindling. Hermann stumbled over some of his beloved books, which had been tossed through the closed kitchen window. He picked one up, carefully removing small pieces of glass. Some pages were torn, but the binding was still intact. He looked up. "Damn them to hell!" he muttered.

"Dad, what's the matter?" Helen asked. Hermann pointed to the plaque. Punctured by bullets, it hung lopsided on the stucco wall. Chunks of cement had piled up on the ground below.

"The whole place is torn apart," Rosa hollered through the shattered kitchen window. "Those miscreants smashed our dishes, tore the curtains, and defecated in our beds."

Everyone joined in the cleanup process. Bessie discovered the empty rain barrels down the incline behind the house, along with the empty water cans; two had been used for target practice and were now useless.

"We must get water." Helen and Paul stacked the remaining functional can on the decrepit cart.

"Wait a minute." Hermann walked over to the well.

"Dad, you're wasting your time. That well has been dry for years. Come on, Paul, let's go." Helen reached for the handle, and they headed down the path.

Hermann fiercely worked the pump. The rain bounced off his head, ran down his face, and seeped into his mouth.

"Come on," he muttered. There was a sputtering, and gobs of mud spewed from the spout. He kept pumping until he thought his arm would fall off, and the mud and sludge slowly changed into sparkling, clear water. It flowed in a steady stream that spilled over the edge where it glistened like diamonds. He stuck his head beneath the spout and opened his mouth. He took big gulps of the cool liquid. He looked up and grinned from ear to ear.

"I need a bucket here," his voice thundered through the air. Rosa stuck her head through the door.

"It's a miracle!" she cried, grabbed the dented stockpot, and hurried outside.

"Don't stop for one second. Keep pumping. Helen, we've got water!" she shouted, her voice rang out loud and powerful. She gave Hermann a quick hug and then relieved him at the pump.

Helen jumped into the air and cheered with her fist raised high. Paul had already turned the cart around and was running back dragging it behind him. The water can bounced around in the cart. They filled the can, the rain barrels, and any vessels Rosa could find that were still usable. It finally stopped raining, and by late afternoon, the laundry hung on the line. The whole house had been scrubbed clean. Everyone had a good wash, the first one in over a week, and the kids wore clean clothes. Most of the adults' clothes had disappeared. Hermann sat draped in a blanket waiting for his pants to dry.

Rosa had cooked an indefinable soup for supper. When they asked her, she refused to divulge the ingredients. They didn't much care anyway, because it was the best soup they had eaten in a long time.

The next morning brought a more gentle rain that lingered in shiny beads on the leaves of the jasmine; a light breeze carried its fragrance back to the little house. Helen inhaled deeply as she sipped weak tea from a cup without a handle, one of two that had survived the looting. Three little finches playfully chased each other through the boxwood hedge below the porch. Her eyes scanned the horizon. Wildenheim lay wrapped in a gray mist. The sun's rays began to push through the clouds and created lacy patches that drifted above the ridgeline.

"We must go into town and find out if we still have a home to return to." Rosa stood in the doorway.

"I know." The sun caressed her face, yet Helen felt a chill.

"We're running out of food." Rosa paused. "For once, we have plenty of water," she added with a chuckle.

"I'll wake Paul, and we'll go into town and check things out." Helen put down her cup.

"I'll heat up some soup for breakfast." Rosa busied herself in the kitchen. Half an hour later, Helen and Paul passed through the gate and turned left, taking the shortcut down the hill. When they arrived at the stream, Paul glanced at the empty cave, wondering if the Gypsies would return. They merged onto the main road where they joined a group of women and children heading back to town. Helen noticed their smiling faces as they chatted and walked with a brisk gait. Occasional laughter rang out. They were a sorry-looking bunch—*Nothing but skinny ragamuffins*, Helen thought—and yet they marched on in the face of defeat, making conversation as if they were taking a Sunday walk in the park. Some of the women carried infants, and others led small children by their hands. She wondered about Fritz who, like the men in their families, was off fighting in the war, his fate unknown. Helen swallowed hard; she would worry about Fritz later. She must concentrate on the survival of her family.

"Do you think our house is still standing?" Paul asked.

"I don't know." Helen pondered their future. What would they do if their home was destroyed? They were at the end of their resources, and she felt her courage waning as a paralyzing fear dominated her thoughts. She glanced at her son. He mustn't sense her anxiety.

The streets were empty as they entered the fringes of town and swerved into Ludwigstrasse. They kept to the left side and worked their way down it. The destruction was devastating. An entire block had been leveled. Scorched timbers and debris piled on top of concrete heaps were the only remains of the homes of some of their neighbors. She observed disturbing tokens of the civilian casualties—a torn jacket or a battered saucepan—yet farther down the street, several houses stood unharmed.

They crossed Ludwigstrasse, climbing over a downed poplar tree, and stared at the empty house that was their home. The windows had been reduced to gaping holes. Jagged cracks dotted the walls and expanded into sloppy spiderwebs. Piles of rubble littered the front yard.

"The walls look like Swiss cheese," Paul commented dryly, and Helen laughed hysterically. Paul stared at his mother. Her whole body convulsed with shrill laughter. He shook her arm, and she stopped abruptly.

"At least the roof is unharmed," she said in calm voice. "Let's go in and board up the windows before we get more rain." They climbed the front stairs and stepped into the vestibule. Helen unlocked the front door to their apartment. A gray layer of dust covered the floor and furniture. Chunks of plaster crowded the living room carpet. The painting of the Fuhrer on the dining room wall hung upside down, and the dishes in the china cabinet had come crashing down. Helen quickly surveyed each room; the damage was tolerable. They blocked the windows as best they could and decided to return to Hermann's Ruhe immediately. As they were leaving, Paul found a jar of peaches, and they gulped them down.

They walked at a steady pace; but for the whisperings of wind and rain, the stillness was complete. They took the shortcut through the woods. The damp exhalation of the pine-needles covering the ground, filled their senses with aromatic fragrance. They passed the Gypsy cave and crossed the stream. Hermann's Ruhe beckoned from above. The kerosene lamp Rosa had placed on the porch railing glittered in the starless night.

3

The Poplar Tree

Eight long days of continuous artillery attacks had all but leveled Wildenheim, forcing the town's capitulation on the third day of April 1945. Oblivious to the destruction, spring had arrived with gusto. A colorful array of wildflowers sprouted defiantly amid the shambles; the colors contrasted starkly with the ruins.

A convoy of slow-moving trucks and armored tanks thundered into town, accompanied by weary soldiers walking single file on Ludwigstrasse. The ground vibrated beneath the crowd of women, children, and old men who had gathered, watching dispassionately. The occupation had begun, and there were no promises forthcoming of an easing of hardships. They had lost most of their possessions and witnessed their friends and neighbors die, but somehow, they had survived. A change of regime did not faze them.

Presence at military events used to be mandatory. The Gestapo would canvass their homes, and anyone found lingering behind was severely punished. The people gathered today, however, had come of their own volition and quickly realized that there was something different about these soldiers. They appeared less threatening. They tossed candy and chewing gum into the crowd, and grinned as they watched the children dive for the treats.

Anne clutched her mother's skirt and watched with dismay. The grinding tanks looked like the gigantic beasts that threatened to devour little children in one of her storybooks. Her face brightened when Paul caught a chocolate bar and shared it with his sisters.

"Mutti, look at Anne," Paul said with a chuckle. Anne cautiously inspected the strange treat and then popped it into her mouth. Her face dissolved into a huge grin as she smacked her lips. She had never tasted chocolate before.

Helen stood quietly. She wore a faded dress that had been taken in several times. The soles of her low-heel leather pumps were paper thin and full of holes. She took off her glasses and wiped her eyes. Anne looked up at her mother and frowned. Her mother was crying again. She cried often these days. Anne had noticed that all the adults around her were sad, their faces lined with worry. She didn't understand why, but it frightened her. She often had nightmares in which fire-breathing dragons swept down and chased her as she kept running until she woke up crying, and her mother came, picked her up, and carried her to her bedroom, a haven, where Anne swiftly drifted off into a dreamless sleep.

The line of soldiers passing them appeared to be endless. Helen tightened her grip on Anne's hand as she speculated about the changes that the arrival of American troops would bring. Like everyone else, she navigated in a daily survival mode and did not think far beyond. It was a relief not to have to seek out the crowded air shelter in the middle of the night any longer, but hunger was a daily caller. They were running out of resources and desperately needed food and fuel.

"Mutti, maybe Papa will be coming home soon." Paul's cheeks were flushed as he watched the parade. He had narrowly missed the obligatory induction into the Hitler Youth, and Helen was grateful for that. So many young boys in that group had been called to active duty by the Fuhrer; their fate uncertain and their future bleak. Their mothers feared the worst.

"I pray your father is still alive," Helen whispered.

"He's alive; I know it," Paul said confidently. "One day, he'll show up; you just wait and see."

Helen didn't know of her husband's whereabouts. The last time he was home on leave, Anne wasn't quite a year old. His most recent letter had reached her thirteen months earlier. There had been no return address. The bits and pieces of news they had gleaned were anything but encouraging, as they learned that the war in Russia had been going badly for the German army. They weren't told that the brutal weather had become a powerful ally for the well-equipped Russian military, whereas the German soldiers lacked the protective gear that would have shielded them from the elements. More men had succumbed to the subzero temperatures in Russia than were killed in action, their frozen bodies left in the fields. They had died oblivious to the horror their families faced at home.

While the German people were starving, the Fuhrer entertained his Nazi cronies in style at the Berghof, his fancy house in Obersalzberg in the Bavarian Alps. The Fuhrer had filled his opulent mansion with priceless artwork confiscated from museums and art galleries. The guests were served the finest food on exquisite china. They worshipped a deranged man who talked about global domination by his armies, and they cheered his prediction of victory.

"I'm hungry." Bessie tugged her mother's arm. When Helen didn't answer, she pulled the tattered sweater that used to belong to her mother tightly around her. "I'm cold," she said.

Helen put her arm around Bessie's shoulders. "I know, dear." She sighed deeply. The kids were always hungry—cold and hungry. She scraped together meals from the most bizarre sources for her family. Rosa was an expert on botany and herbage and made daily excursions into the nearby forest, which yielded mushrooms, berries, nuts, and all kinds of odd-shaped plants that were cooked into soups and stews.

Occasionally, Hermann was able to trap a rabbit, which provided a more fundamental change in menu. Nothing was wasted, including the fur, which Helen tailored into warm mittens and hats for the children.

"Let's go," Helen said as she glanced at the sky. The sun had disappeared behind a cloud formation that rolled in quickly. "Looks like we're going to get some rain."

Packed with violence, the storm descended upon the sleeping town. Rapid lightning and crashing thunder brought drenching rain and hail the size of walnuts that bounced off the roof like ping-pong balls. The branches of the tall poplar trees lining both sides of Ludwigstrasse writhed in protest as strong gusts ripped through them. A muddy torrent swallowed the street and expanded across the sidewalks.

Light flashes invaded the room. Paul stirred and jerked his head. He strained to hear. The thunder roared into another explosive peak. He jumped out of bed. His heart was pounding, and beads of perspiration appeared on his forehead. The rain thrashed against the windowpane. His eyes followed the flickering shadows that raced across the wall, and he slumped on the edge of the bed. He was wide-awake now, and relief penetrated his consciousness. The war was over. The planes would never come again. *I'm not afraid.* He mouthed the words defiantly. He shivered and crawled back beneath the covers.

He glanced across the room where Bessie slept soundly. Anne had already deserted her bed to seek refuge with her mother.

Paul wondered whether it was the storm or another nightmare that had roused her this particular night. The jaunts across the hall to be with her mother occurred frequently, and Paul believed that his mother was far too indulgent. After all, Anne was five years old and should sleep in her own bed...nightmares or not.

Nothing ever woke Bessie. Her face was relaxed as she snored softly, her hair draped across the pillow like a halo. A faint smile hovered around her lips. *I bet she's dreaming about food again,* Paul thought. There was so little of it these days. Their meals were scanty, and except for the kitchen, the apartment was always cold. Wood was scarce. Since the war had ended, coal was once more available in limited quantities, but the price was way beyond their means.

To help keep them alive, his mother had been trading family heirlooms and even her jewelry for food. Paul's thoughts wandered back to the time when he had accompanied her on one of her "shopping excursions." She had used the phrase sarcastically. It was a foggy morning when they walked down Ludwigstrasse. The bridge had long since been blown up, and they had to climb down the steep bank until they reached the railroad tracks below only to discover that they were flooded from the recent rain. They trudged through the ankle-deep current and scrambled up the hill on the other side. Their shoes squealed and sputtered with each step.

They walked past the outskirts of town and across an empty field; when they reached a clump of conifers, they followed a narrow path. It wound through low shrubs and led to a wooden shack. Iron bars fortified the empty spaces that used to be windows. Rusty steel plates pieced together made up the front door. It reminded Paul of the artwork by a man named Picasso he had learned about in school right before the bombs blew up the building one night; classes had been in recess ever since.

Helen banged on the steel door with her fist. Someone opened it just wide enough to allow them to squeeze through. The kerosene lamp did little for illumination, but once his eyes had had a chance to adjust, Paul noticed a swarthy middle-aged man.

"Hello, darling," the man greeted Helen and ignored Paul. His obnoxious grin revealed blackened teeth. Paul resented how the man's eyes swept over his mother. He detected a foreign accent and wondered why he wasn't fighting in the war, like all the other men his age.

The shack consisted of one room lined with shelves and stacked with boxes. There was a nasty smell, and Paul wrinkled his nose. A faint noise at his feet made him aware of a scrawny cat rubbing against his leg. He reached down to pet it, but it drew back and hissed viciously.

"You don't want to mess with Lucifer. He's my rat catcher. You should see him attack and devour his prey; it's a mean sport." The man threw back his head in a roaring guffaw and then stopped abruptly and turned to Helen.

"Well, sweet lady, what have you brought me today?"

Helen pulled a white handkerchief from her purse and unfolded it in her palm, revealing a ring set with a large marquise garnet stone surrounded by pearls and a bracelet of garnets set in a continuous floral design. Paul remembered seeing Rosa wear the ring and bracelet on special occasions, and he opened his mouth to speak, but Helen jammed her elbow into his ribs.

The man picked up the ring and examined it carefully, and then he checked out the bracelet. He seemed to be more impressed with the bracelet and snorted his approval. He walked toward a small table in the middle of the room, rummaged through a drawer, and pulled out a loupe.

"This jewelry is fourteen-carat gold. The pearls are real, and the garnet stones are of the highest quality," Helen said. Paul noticed a slight quiver in her voice.

"That may be true, but as it stands, you're in no position to negotiate, unless, of course..."

"No, no, for the last time, no." Helen stamped her foot. He stared at her boldly, his mouth twisted into a cruel smile.

"Because I like you, I will give you one five-pound bag each of flour, sugar, and a box of tea," he said.

Helen opened her mouth to protest, but he added, "Wait, there is something else. He opened one of the boxes on the floor, pulled out a brown cardboard container, and pushed it in her face. "I'll throw in one of these."

Helen examined the small rectangular box that weighed about a pound. There was black writing across the front. Paul looked over her shoulder and said, "That's written in English."

"Aren't you the clever one?" the man mocked.

"What's inside?" Helen demanded.

"Powdered egg. I only have one crate of this stuff, and I am giving one to you because I'm feeling generous." He reached out to touch her face, and Helen shrank back.

"But...the jewelry is worth so much more..." There were tears in her eyes. When Rosa had come to her with the ring and bracelet, she didn't want to take them, but she had traded in all of her own jewelry already, including her wedding ring, and Rosa had insisted.

"We need the food; we don't want to end up as ornamented corpses," she said.

Helen looked up at the man and shook her head.

"This is the best I can do..." he said. There was a knock on the door, and he said impatiently, "What is it, yes or no? I have other customers to take care of."

So they took the food and left. It was enough to guarantee survival for a little while longer.

The rain hit the windowpane in a steady rhythm. Paul was unable to go back to sleep. A soft chuckle escaped from his lips as he recalled the events of the evening. After dinner, the family remained in the warm kitchen and played one of their favorite games where each person made up a story. Bessie's stories were endless, and she reveled in having everyone's attention. Hermann's humorous tales often had them in stitches, whereas Paul delighted in delivering haunting accounts of ghosts and evil spirits with such realistic animation that Anne screamed in terror, while Bessie hammered him with her fists. He had grinned broadly at his mother's signal to tone it down.

Across the hall, Anne woke briefly and listened to the rain. She snuggled against her mother in the big bed. Her father was at war, and she was glad he was gone. She had no memory of him, but her mother talked about him every day. There was a framed picture of a dark-haired man on the dresser. She often watched her mother pick up the photo and hug it to her chest as tears trickled down her face. Anne resented the man in the photo for making her mother cry.

Anne was confused by the anxiety surrounding her. It was her grandfather who always made her feel safe. He encouraged her to dream and play, even be silly if she felt like it, but above all, he let her win at chess. When he introduced her to the game, she took to it with a passion and showed a great aptitude for planning her strategies. Next to her mother, Anne loved spending time with her grandfather more than with anyone else.

Paul counted the seconds between each lightning flash and the thunderbolts that followed. The storm still lingered directly above the town. The deep rumbling sounds faded briefly, and he heard a distinctive crash. He jumped out of bed and dressed quickly. He pulled his slicker over his head, grabbed his boots, and nudged his sister not too gently. "Wake up, Bessie."

She opened her eyes and stared at him in fearful confusion. "The airplanes..."

"No, silly. A tree went down. Wake Mutti and Opa. I'm heading outside." He ran out the door. In the stairway, he almost collided with Mr. Stringer, who was clutching an ax. A baggy rain poncho hung crookedly across his scrawny body and covered most of his knee-high boots.

"Paul, get the saw. Hurry." Mr. Stringer's voice trembled with excitement. "I think it's a big one."

Paul dashed down the basement steps, retrieved the single-handle metal saw from their storage room, and hurried to catch up with Mr. Stringer.

As he stepped outside, he was pelted with strong rain gusts that seemed determined to hold him back. He fought his way down the steps, ignoring the sharp teeth of the saw clamoring for his thigh. A flash of lighting highlighted the large poplar tree stretched across the street. It had created a barrier that confined the water into a shadowy lake that invaded the front yards nearby. Mr. Stringer began stripping the branches, and Paul attacked the tree trunk with his saw, as several neighbors showed up.

Since Mr. Stringer had been the first person to arrive at the scene, he took charge of the operation. He judged the size of the tree and declared that there was enough wood for five people. They continued to work without further comment, as the other neighbors left. The wood was precious, but they knew it was not enough for all of them. They were disappointed but respected the rules. The rain whipped their backs as they shuffled through the muddy water back to their homes where it was cold but dry.

Helen appeared at the tree site pushing Anne's old baby carriage, a useful standby that had come in handy on many occasions for hauling all kinds of stuff. Mary and Hermann were right behind her. Hermann carried a large, bright coral canvas bag, made by Rosa from the remnants of a parachute he had found in the forest. They loaded up the wood. By sunrise, all evidence of the fallen tree was gone; not even a twig was left behind.

After the wood had been stored, Helen invited the Stringers for a cup of tea. Mrs. Stringer had already joined Rosa in the kitchen. The unexpected windfall created a cheerful mood as they gathered around the blazing fire in the kitchen stove. The first appearance of daylight crept through the window and found the group deep in conversation. Their clothes had dried, and they savored the warmth in the kitchen. They should all be dead tired. They had worked through the night in the drenching rain, but there was a reluctance to break up the gathering.

The doorbell rang—incessantly. Angry voices penetrated the front door. The people in the kitchen sat in silence. Helen rose reluctantly, but Hermann placed his hand on her arm.

"Let me take care of this."

"No, I'll go." She walked out of the kitchen into the hallway and opened the door. She cringed when she looked into the flushed faces of her landlords, who screamed at her in unison. Helen covered her ears. "One at a time, please." Mrs. Brenner clamped her thin lips together, and fixed her eyes on Helen in an evil stare.

"There is wet wood in the basement lockers. You know very well that I do not allow wet wood in the house," Mr. Brenner said with labored breath.

His wife quickly added, "You people always make trouble; if it isn't those brats of yours, it's something else." Her head bobbed up and down on an invisible neck, obstructed by the many layers of her sagging chin.

The Brenners were the only family on the block that regularly got coal delivered. Their brownnosing with the current powers in charge resulted in many benefits as evidenced in the circumference of their huge bellies. Before the war, Mr. Brenner had been the chief of police in Wildenheim and a zealous member of the Nazi Party. Once the Allied occupation had begun, his loyalty shifted to the new regime with the same zeal that he had shown Adolf Hitler, and he provided the occupational forces with information that only he, as former chief of police, had been privy to.

In the hallway, Helen was joined by the rest of the group, and there was a chorus of outraged voices. Hermann raised his fists and threatened to belt Mr. Brenner. Helen stamped her foot and shouted, "Quiet!"

She took a deep breath and said, "What do you want from us?" Before Mr. Brenner could reply, she continued, "We need the wood desperately. Will you allow us to keep the wood if we share it with you?" She turned around and faced the Stringers, her eyes pleading. Mr. Stringer directed a grim glance at his wife and daughter-in-law who nodded in silent resignation.

"You may have some of our wood as well..." Mr. Stringer hesitated. His eyes lit up, and he grinned wickedly. "There's one condition." Mrs. Brenner opened her mouth to speak, but Mr. Stringer kept on talking. "From now on, you'll allow the children to roller-skate on the driveway."

Mr. Brenner gulped. "That's out of the question. The horrible noise will give my wife a headache..."

Mr. Stringer's wife had remained silent but now stepped forward and announced, "No roller-skating, no wood."

Mrs. Brenner's jaw dropped in the face of such open defiance. Her lips drew back from her teeth until her mouth resembled that of a vicious dog. "All right, they can roller-skate, but only on Wednesdays," she snarled.

"Hurray!" Paul's and Elisabeth's outcries were reverberating through the stairway, when a piercing scream silenced everyone. They turned to face little Anne who had tiptoed down the hallway to investigate the commotion.

"Anne, what's the matter?" Helen picked up her daughter.

"I don't have any roller skates." She began to sob and buried her face in her mother's sweater.

Her brother and sister had inherited their parents' skates, but there had never been an opportunity to use them. The children were forbidden to skate in the street, and the long concrete driveway was off-limits. Anne visualized her brother and sister having a ball skating while she could only watch from the cold sandstone steps. She threw back her head and howled.

Mary Stringer smiled and said, "Don't cry, sweetheart. I've got a pair of skates. They can be adjusted to fit you."

Anne's tearstained face beamed and she clapped her hands.

"That's settled, then." Mr. Stringer turned and led the way back into the kitchen.

"You'll get your wood tomorrow," Hermann growled and slammed the door in their faces.

Rosa refilled the kettle on the stove, while Helen sent the children back to bed.

"What a brilliant idea." Rosa patted Mr. Stringer on the arm. He smiled with pleasure.

"I know how those kids love to skate. All these restrictions are ridiculous. The Brenners should remember their own childhood."

"I don't believe they had one." Helen poured the tea. Their laughter lingered in the kitchen.

From that day on, life took on a new meaning for Anne. Each Wednesday, at dawn, wearing Mary Stringer's old skates, she tried to master remaining in a vertical position while rolling along on the concrete slab. Her brother and sister often joined her. Bessie lost interest quickly and searched for new adventures, but Paul rediscovered his passion for skating and proved to be a patient teacher to Anne. She learned quickly in spite of making repeated contact with the unforgiving concrete. Her knees were often bloodied to the point where Helen made her soak in the bathtub with her clothes on in order to separate her pants from the wounds without causing excruciating pain.

Helen sat on the sandstone steps and watched proudly as Paul and Anne glided past her with ease. Paul executed fancy footwork that culminated in a respectable spin.

"Mutti, watch me!" Anne shouted as she whizzed by. Helen smiled. The children had forgotten about war, hunger, and fear, and they had fun doing simple things children should be doing. The war had for so long crowded out everything in their lives. She raised her head; the sun had pushed through the clouds. Spring had finally arrived, and the branches of the poplar trees were sprouting green buds. She inhaled deeply; the air was sweet and fresh.

The curtains moved behind the second-floor window where Mrs. Brenner had pressed her pudgy nose against the glass pane and glared at her happy tenants.

4

The Warehouse

The feel of autumn invaded the air. The oaks and beech trees had begun their transformation, as the bright green of the leaves faded and gold-yellow and red pigments took control. The harvest moon loomed in the inky sky, and fragments of moonbeams skipped from branches to tree trunks where they glittered like opals, and then they were gone. They reminded Helen of the elusive fireflies she used to chase when she was a child.

The peace and tranquility in the forest was profound as the three people walked in silence beneath the tall trees. The carpet of leaves and pine needles soft-pedaled the creaky wheels of the old wooden cart.

Perched on a gnarled branch, a spotted owl focused on the group below but soon lost interest. Paul squinted in the darkness. The outline of a large building rose between the trees. His heart began to beat a little faster as they came closer. He put his hand on Helen's arm, and they paused. He gently tilted the handle against the cart. A few yards away, a chain-link fence stretched across the rear of the structure and followed the edge of the property. The Americans had repurposed the building into a warehouse. A gigantic security beam lit up the yard and part of the roof, but dark shadows cloaked the rear of the building.

"We'll leave the cart here behind these bushes," Paul whispered.

"Bessie, you'll stay with the cart," Helen said.

They advanced cautiously. Helen observed the large building and marveled that it had escaped destruction, while directly across from it stood the shell of what used to be a quaint restaurant. Bathed in the bright light, she clearly saw the remnants of the outside walls, surrounded by wreckage and burned timbers, a sad reminder of the happy times spent there so long ago. The memory of the last May Fest they had celebrated there was as strong as the fragrant night air that invaded Helen's senses with the magic of days long gone. She could almost hear the beat of the music played by the three-man band. They played tirelessly as she whirled with Fritz across the dance floor. They danced to the waltz, foxtrot, and everyone's favorite, the polka. Large wreaths of pine and fresh-cut flowers hung on the front walls of the dance hall; their colorful ribbons fluttered in the breeze. Tables and chairs clustered around the mighty oak tree in the center of the yard. Garlands of multicolored lights strung across its lower branches set the tone for the guests.

Helen blinked away the memories. There was no time to dwell on the past. She stared at the grim wall. The three narrow windows facing them were grimy, but there were no metal bars. Paul had watched her and nodded his head. "No bars; the windows are too small for anyone to crawl through. Even Anne couldn't squeeze through them."

Helen thought about her youngest daughter safely asleep at home with her grandparents watching over her. Waves of doubt and guilt assailed her. The severity of their scheme and the threat it invited could have serious consequences. She shrugged off all misgivings. She had made her decision, and there was no turning back now.

"I've noticed that they keep the door of the warehouse unlocked. The guard goes in there when it rains." Paul spoke rapidly.

"Once I'm inside, I'll open the window on the far left and pitch the stuff to you."

"But the guards…" Helen worried.

"There's only one guard," Paul assured her. "I've watched him for several nights now. He walks around the perimeter a couple of times and then settles down for a nap on the bench over there by the ruins. Don't worry; I'll make sure it's safe before I head for the door." He pulled the dark-green knitted cap he was wearing down onto his face. "Okay, I'm ready…"

"Wait…" Helen's hushed voice ebbed into the night; Paul was already gone. She moved closer and crouched low. She craned her head and focused on the building. Everything they so desperately needed was behind those walls: flour, sugar, canned goods, and maybe even soap. She and Rosa made their own soap, but because they lacked the ingredients to add fragrance and soften the texture, it was coarse and the children complained that it smelled of lard.

Their situation had become desperate. There had been two suicides in the neighborhood; an elderly couple was found dead in their beds. Helen remembered seeing them walking up Ludwigstrasse holding hands. They would always stop and chat, and inquire about Fritz, encouraging her to never give up hope. They had left a note behind saying that they were too tired and too hungry to go on. Helen was saddened at the news but vowed that her family's fate would be survival. If this mission proved to be successful, they could hang on for a little while longer, at least until the Allied forces managed to create some kind of order and brought in the food supplies as they had promised.

She heard voices and crept closer; she bumped into Paul.

"There are two guards," he hissed through gritted teeth.

Helen blanched. "We'll have to forget about it and get out of here. It's too dangerous." Her voice trembled.

"Let's wait and see. We've come this far…"

"The risks have just doubled. They'll shoot us without hesitation." Helen was backing through the brush, when she heard women's laughter. She paused.

Paul turned and said, "Two women just showed up."

They inched their way up to the fence and peered across the yard. The women and the two soldiers had gathered by the wooden bench. They were involved in animated discussion, and after a few minutes, one of the soldiers walked across the yard and flung open the door to the warehouse. There were shuffling noises and the sound of boxes dropping. The remaining soldier offered the women his cigarette pack, and they sat down on the bench. Wreaths of cigarette smoke twirled playfully in the light as the soldier emerged from the warehouse carrying a brown cardboard box, which he placed on the ground in front of the women. He pulled out a bottle of whiskey and passed it around. The women giggled and took several swigs. The soldier stepped back and pointed to the box. The women squatted on the ground and pulled out each item. Helen spotted bags and boxes of various sizes, tin cans, and individual cigarette packs. The women seemed pleased and indicated their approval. They placed the contents back into the box, and one of the soldiers pulled one woman to him and kissed her.

Helen frowned and looked at Paul. He was fifteen going on sixteen and had surpassed everyone in the family in height. His resemblance to Fritz was incredible, including his voice, which had deepened. War had forced Paul to relinquish many of his childhood patterns and adopt those of an adult more quickly than she had wanted. He showed his maturity in the way he stepped up to support the family in dealing with the chaos and confusion war had thrust upon them.

At this moment, Paul's eyes were fearless and sparkled with anticipation, and Helen worried that he could consider this mission an adventure and minimize the seriousness of the situation. She had opened her mouth to speak when he said, "This little interlude is just what we needed. Hopefully, they'll get good and drunk, and then we can accomplish what we came for without any interference."

Helen nodded and squeezed his hand. She crawled back to check on Bessie and found her asleep in the cart. She covered her with one of the canvas potato sacks and returned to join Paul.

"One of them disappeared with one of the girls behind the ruins," he said softly, his eyes narrowing.

Helen kept watching the scene in front of her. The other soldier sat on the bench with one of the girls cuddled on his lap. They were laughing and taking turns drinking from the bottle; suddenly, he reached up and hurled it at the large oak tree. Shards of tiny crystals gathered at the bottom of the trunk. The girl giggled and jumped off his lap. She lifted her skirt and played at adjusting an imaginary nylon stocking. For a long moment, the soldier's gaze lingered on her shapely legs, and then he turned and staggered across the yard and into the warehouse.

Helen studied the woman. She was pretty with medium-length blond hair. Helen guessed her age to be in the early thirties. She appeared to be quite sober as she paced up and down. When the soldier returned, she stretched out her arms, and he fell into them, raising the bottle of whiskey way up high. She snatched it from him and drank deeply. When he leaned closer for a kiss, she quickly handed him the bottle.

Helen watched the scene with sadness. They were all here for the same reason. Hunger drove this woman and her friend. Their families suffered just like hers. How much had she taken for granted until this terrible war happened? She shuddered at the idea of having turned into a criminal who at this moment was in the process of robbing a guarded warehouse at substantial risk, and had involved her children to assist in the plot. She fidgeted as she checked her wrist. It was a habit. There was no watch. It had long since been traded for food. Fritz had given it to her on her thirtieth birthday. It was a beautiful watch with two oval-cut peridot, her birthstone. Their clear, translucent color had always reminded her of Fritz's eyes. What would he say if he saw her this night?

Shrill laughter preceded the second woman's emergence from behind the ruins. She appeared in a state of dishabille. Her hair was mussed, and her blouse torn. She walked toward the two people who were sitting on the bench, and took the whiskey bottle from the soldier. Pretending to raise it to her lips, she swung it high and brought it down on his head. The soldier collapsed like an accordion. The women quickly picked up the box and without looking back vanished into the forest. Helen and Paul waited and watched, holding their breaths. A deadly silence hung across the yard.

"This is our chance." Before Helen could answer, Paul had jumped across the fence, and advanced stealthily toward the front of the warehouse where he disappeared from view. Helen hurried to retrieve the canvas sacks. She woke Bessie, and together, they took their positions beneath the window Paul had opened. He tossed small cartons, tin cans, and brown paper packages into the bushes. Helen and Bessie stuffed the potato sacks as fast as they could and loaded them onto the cart.

"Paul, that's enough. Get out of there. Now!" Helen urged as she glanced around the corner of the warehouse. The soldier lay curled on the ground. He did not stir. She wondered briefly what had happened to the other guy.

"Just a minute. I believe these are cigars. Opa will be thrilled." Paul's voice was muffled.

The sound of an approaching vehicle roared through the night, its headlights caught the trees heavy with leaves that were now restlessly moving. Helen and Bessie dropped on the soft, damp ground. Helen's heart thumped like drumbeats as she focused on the yard. The jeep had come to a halt by the giant oak tree. Two soldiers jumped out, and one of them ran over and examined the body on the ground. The injured soldier stirred. Blood streamed down his face. The second soldier ran inside the warehouse.

Paul. Helen mouthed his name. Her legs trembled under her.

"Mutti, Paul's still inside…"

Helen quickly clamped her hand across Bessie's mouth.

"Hush." She watched anxiously as the soldier reappeared, walked over to the injured GI, and reached into his pants pocket. He retrieved the key and proceeded to lock the heavy wooden door, pocketing the key. Paul was trapped inside the warehouse. Helen cowered on the ground with Bessie huddled close to her.

Across the yard, the battered soldier had regained consciousness. He sat on the bench; blood was dripping down his face. The other soldier appeared from behind the ruins, a body slung over his shoulder. Helen felt her stomach churn when she saw the bloody head. He deposited the body on the ground and spoke urgently into his radio.

Helen realized that they had to leave at once before the whole place was crawling with soldiers. Unless they decided to search the warehouse, Paul was safe inside for the time being. She took Bessie's hand, and they crept toward the cart. They grabbed the handle, and together they struggled to pull the rickety cart through the forest. A strong wind had risen; its powerful scream drowned out all other sounds. They reached the edge of the forest and almost collided with a man who stepped in front of them.

"Helen, it's me." Hermann's urgent whisper made her breathe a sigh of relief.

At that moment, a vehicle raced across the narrow road toward the warehouse. The sirens and flashing red lights sent the animals scrambling. Birds screeched as they rose from their nests. The three people left the forest and hurried along the deserted road.

"Please tell me that Paul's all right?" Hermann said as they arrived at the house. She gave one silent nod, and Hermann frowned when he observed her quivering lips and the tears in her eyes.

Rosa had joined them in unloading the cart. "We'll have to hurry before the Brenners discover us," she said. With Bessie's help, she lifted the last sack, and they struggled up the steps.

Helen and Hermann carried the empty cart into the backyard. Sweat poured down his face, and Helen's arms ached in protest of the heavy load. Step by slow, agonizing step, they inched forward. They lowered the cart onto the cement driveway repeatedly for a quick break. When they reached the vegetable garden, they deposited the cart behind the peach tree and snuck back to the house.

Hermann wiped his brow, and Helen fell into a kitchen chair while Rosa put the kettle on the stove.

"Mutti, I'm going to bed." Bessie yawned.

"Good night, sweetheart. Try not to wake your sister." Helen hugged Bessie to her. "Thanks for your help tonight." Bessie nodded sleepily and trudged down the long hallway to the children's bedroom.

"Where is Paul? What happened?" Rosa poured tea into mismatched cups.

"He's inside the warehouse…trapped." Helen's voice caught, and she began to weep. "I should have never agreed to this. It's all my fault."

"Look, we had made this decision together, and we knew that there would be risks. Stop blaming yourself and tell us exactly what happened," Rosa said firmly.

Helen wiped her faced and said, "Everything was going well until…"

Paul peered out the window. Several vehicles had arrived. The whole yard was buzzing with soldiers. The MP had thrown a blanket across the body of the soldier stretched out on the ground, and the injured GI had been taken away via ambulance. Paul advanced softly to the rear window. He squinted as he searched the forest. There was no sign of Helen or Bessie. He dropped down on a stack of small boxes. He was on his own and felt a sense of isolation that was almost painful. He must remain calm and examine his options. There had to be a way out of this place. He could bang on the door and make his presence known, but what would they do to him? Beat him up and throw him in prison? Or maybe even shoot him? He fidgeted with his cap and then pulled it off his head and ran his fingers through his cropped hair.

Motors whirred. He ran to the window. The convoy of jeeps was leaving. One soldier remained and stood at attention. The vehicles disappeared in a squall of leaves and pebbles. The remaining soldier began pacing the yard.

Well, that's it for tonight, thought Paul. He tiptoed to the rear window. The high light beam spread ghostly images upon the trees. He turned and looked around. Hunger pangs stabbed at his stomach, and he decided to investigate the food supply in front of him. He took off his shoes and moved around soundlessly. When he opened one of the large cardboard boxes, he found dozens of key-opening cans. He marveled at the genius of the Americans and the way they preserved their food as he opened the can and stared at a concoction of meat and potato hash. He dipped his finger into it and licked it. Cold, but tasty. He devoured three cans and then searched through other boxes. He pulled out a small package containing ten chocolate bars. He ate them all and then arranged several large cartons into a makeshift chair onto which he reclined, stretching his legs way out. He shivered, put his cap back over his hair, and pulled his jacket tightly around his chest. Tomorrow, he would figure out his escape. He relaxed, and his eyelids got heavy; he wondered if he had included a box of chocolate bars in the stuff he had handed to his mother. He couldn't remember. His head dropped, and he drifted into a deep, dreamless sleep.

"…and that's exactly what happened." Helen blew her nose. Rosa and Hermann sat in silence. A chill invaded the small kitchen as the dying fire sent its last crackling gusts up the chimney.

"There must be a way to get Paul out of there," Hermann finally said.

"We could always go to the Americans and tell them the truth," Rosa offered, but her husband and daughter shook their heads emphatically.

"After all, he's just a boy," Rosa insisted. "What can they do to him?"

"Plenty!" Hermann exclaimed.

"He's a child."

"He is old enough to break into the warehouse, which makes him a thief," Hermann said. "There's nothing we can do tonight. Paul is safe for the time being. He's a resourceful boy, who, I'm sure, is sound asleep by now. As we should be. Tomorrow, we'll go there and check out the situation and decide what must be done." Hermann limped though the kitchen door, followed by Rosa and Helen. They passed the sacks of food stacked in the corner without looking at them.

Helen slept fitfully. Fritz's face appeared in front of her. "What have you done to our son?" He spoke with muffled voice, and then his image faded. A ghostly vision of the warehouse rose sharply. Dogs barked viciously and strained at their leashes as they sniffed at the door. She stood at the fence in the back of the building and screamed when she saw Paul's face pressed against the dirty window.

She bolted upright in her bed and stared into the dark. Perspiration trickled down her cheeks and neck. She laid her head back down on the pillow, covered her mouth, and cried herself to sleep.

Bristles brushed against Paul's cheek. He moaned and opened his eyes. His hand reached up to his face, and he watched in horror as a rat ran behind a stack of boxes. He jumped to his feet and followed the direction it had taken. He heard a truck approach, and it came to a stop. Voices echoed through the yard. He crept to the window. It was barely daylight. Two soldiers unloaded several large crates. The guard headed toward the door of the warehouse. Paul looked around in desperation. He quickly grabbed his shoes and the container filled with his trash and raced to the back of the room where boxes were stacked high, separated by a narrow aisle. He moved some of them and squeezed behind. The rat screeched, jumped over his foot, and hid between two crates. Its long, wiry tail wavered briefly and then was whisked out of sight.

The door flung open. Paul held his breath. He heard the soldiers talking as they brought in crates and boxes and deposited them at the other end of the building. Snakes of cigarette smoke slithered in the daylight reaching far inside the warehouse.

A tailgate slammed, and the voices faded away. He raised his head. Light was streaming through the open door. It occurred to him that he could race up to the door in seconds but not without being seen. He rose and tiptoed to the nearest window facing the forest. He gasped when he saw his mother staring at him from across the fence. He was signaling that he was okay when footsteps approached, and he ducked quickly. The door slammed shut, and he heard the turn of the key. The engine revved, and the truck took off. Relieved, he wiped his brow. The rat stuck its head out from between the crates, sniffed the air, and left its hiding place to run down the aisle.

Paul looked through one of the front windows. A soldier reclined on the wooden bench smoking a cigarette, his rifle next to him. Paul turned when his eyes fell on a kerosene lamp placed on two stacked crates, a sleeve of matchboxes next to it. Burned matches littered the floor. He hurried to the rear window. His mother was gone. He released the lock and pushed the narrow window open, stuck his head through and scanned the trees.

"Paul," Helen whispered as she looked up. She stood directly beneath the window; her eyes filled with fear. "We've been so worried. Are you all right?"

"Yes, yes," he assured her. "The rat and I are fine."

"What…"

"Never mind, Mutti. I've got to get out of here. I almost considered making a stab at it a few minutes ago."

"I know, but it would have been too dangerous." Helen's voice was barely audible. "I've brought you some tea. I know there's plenty of food inside, but you may be thirsty." She handed him a thermos.

"Thanks." He noticed the worried expression on her face and nodded reassuringly. He opened the thermos and drank deeply.

Helen smiled bravely back at him. "We're working on a plan to get you out."

"Soldiers arrived today to stock the warehouse. What I'm worried about is when they'll come to pick up supplies," he said. "If they comb the warehouse…" His voice trailed off.

Helen frowned. She had considered confronting the guard and explaining the situation. Surely, they would be sympathetic. Paul had been watching her.

"I know what you're thinking. Don't forget that there was murder committed here last night, which without a doubt, would be blamed on us," he said.

"I know," Helen said. "The news is all over the radio. The surviving soldier gave a description that fits most of the young women around here. The Americans have announced that severe punishment awaits the offenders once they're caught." She frowned. "They have reinforced the guards…two soldiers here and one at the entrance of the road."

Footsteps approached. Helen ducked into the bushes. She held her breath. The guard passed by and continued to walk along the perimeter of the fence. Paul peeked through the edge of the window unable to see the soldier. Helen waved him back and slowly crawled away, careful not to disturb any branches.

She turned into Ludwigstrasse and noticed her father pacing the sidewalk in front of their house, dragging his crippled leg. He appeared agitated.

"Well?" Hermann looked at her expectantly.

Two spots of color flared on her cheekbones. "He's all right," she said. "I spoke with him. He's eaten…has slept…all night." The words came in fractions.

"Helen, he's young and not bogged down by the fears that consume us. What did he say?"

"He sounds good, confident, but he's anxious and wants to get out. I'm going back to the warehouse tonight."

"I'll go with you."

"No, Dad. I may have to make a hasty retreat, and you're in no shape for that."

"Yes, I know," he uttered with a snort.

"The longer he stays in there, the greater the chances of getting caught. I even considered talking to the guard today, but Paul made me realize that it would be a mistake."

"I heard on the radio that several women have been picked up for questioning; however, they had alibis and were released," Hermann said.

"They would have to question most of the young women in town!" Helen exclaimed. "The killing was unfortunate, but I don't blame these women. They're trying to keep their families fed. No one cares what happens to us. If we want to survive, we have to fend for ourselves. Sticking to principles will not keep us alive."

Before Hermann could answer, Helen whispered, "We have no choice. I pray that history will not judge us too harshly."

Hermann nodded.

"Ten years from now, someone will read about us and say, 'How could this woman have been willing to sacrifice her son?'" Helen's voice caught. "I have two daughters as well, and I love them all the same. I would risk my life for all of you without a moment's hesitation. It would be by far the easier thing to do. If anything happens to Paul, my death will come slowly, one second at a time…"

"This damned war has turned us into criminals."

"No, Dad. I think it's a crime what we have to endure. We didn't want this war...and now we must do what is necessary to survive...and deal with the guilt later."

"You have done nothing to feel guilty about."

"Oh, Dad, I am just so tired. If I had to worry about me only, I would end it, I believe..."

"Don't say that, ever." Hermann's voice rose sharply.

"Don't worry. I'm not giving up. I swear to you, whatever it takes, I will fight to my dying breath to keep my family from starvation." She pressed her lips together and walked up the front steps with her head held high.

Paul paced the floor in his stocking feet. He longed for his warm bed. Two nights' sleep on the unforgiving boxes was punishment even for his young body. The rat sat at his feet and stared at him; it had cautiously accepted the intruder who had become an ally. Paul stretched his arms and yawned. He felt dirty and smelly, and although he often protested the daily washing his mother demanded, at this point, he would welcome a warm bath.

Light beams skipped through the windows, and a jeep came to a stop. The guards were changing. He knew the routine by heart. He looked out the window. One soldier climbed out of the jeep while the driver waited with the engine running. The two soldiers chatted a few minutes as they smoked a cigarette. Paul pressed his nose against the window in a daring gesture. Adrenaline pumped through his body. They didn't even look in his direction. He pulled back and sat down. He was tearing the wrapper of a chocolate bar when the sound of the jeep engine faded.

Paul was munching his sweet treat when his eyes fell on the kerosene lamp. He walked toward it and took a closer look; the reservoir was filled. His thoughts raced, and a plan for his escape was born. It was daring and dangerous, but it just might work. Beads of perspiration gathered on his forehead. He stared into the middle distance. Pictures of his family slowly passed in front of his eyes like a movie in slow motion: his mother and father laughing and proud when he caught the monster bass that Sunday afternoon on the river; Anne and Bessie begging him to teach them new moves as they roller-skated on the driveway... He looked up and exhaled sharply. His mind was made up. He slipped into his shoes and checked the front window one more time. The guard was nowhere in sight.

He picked up the lamp and splashed kerosene across the two wooden door panels and a pile of boxes sitting near. He lit the match and threw it at the door. A fire spawned, tongues of flame licked at the door and reached for the stacked crates. Thick smoke filled the air. Paul covered his nose and mouth with his cap and moved back. He tried to stifle his coughs. There was so much smoke.

The door rattled and was pulled open. Greedy flames escaped and climbed up on the roof. The guard retreated and yelled something into his radio. Paul ran from his hiding place, slipped past the guard, and raced toward the fence. He failed to clear the fence and landed on the railing instead, and struggled across. He heard a shot and then another. He fell and collided with his mother.

"Go!"

They ran as fast as they could until they reached the outskirts of the forest. They stopped to catch their breaths. Helen panted while Paul examined his stinging arm. Deep red blood colored his shirtsleeve.

"You're hurt!" Helen cried.

"I'm all right. Let's go home."

They moved quickly in the shadows cast by the eerie ruins and made their way through fields of debris that led them to

Ludwigstrasse. Paul leaned heavily against Helen; his breath came labored and irregular. She was dragging him up the steps when the front door opened. Hermann and Rosa grabbed him. Paul had lost consciousness. They carried him inside and gently laid him on the sofa.

"There's so much blood..." Rosa fussed with Paul's shirt while Hermann got the scissors to cut off the sleeve.

"It's just a flesh wound, but he needs stitches," she whispered.

"The bullet that hit him must have ricocheted after striking a fence post." Helen's voice was shaky. Paul stirred and opened his eyes.

"My arm's killing me."

Helen brushed down an errant cowlick in Paul's hair. "You've been grazed by a bullet. Omi is trying to stop the bleeding," she said softly.

"We need a doctor," Rosa said as she tied the tourniquet.

Helen kneeled at Paul's side. He turned to her and said, "Don't tell me I fainted...did I?"

"Just for a second." Helen smiled reassuringly.

Hermann took her aside. "He needs stitches. If I fetch the doctor, he'll have to report the incident."

"What'll we do?" Helen's worried eyes hung on her father's face.

"Rosa has nursing experience. She used to volunteer at the hospital. She knows how to stitch up the wound."

"We must boil the water. Helen, bring the Steinhager and bandages." Rosa had already made her decision as she rummaged through her sewing box for the proper needle.

"Mother, do you think you can do it?"

"Yes. Just pray very hard. This is my grandson, which complicates things for me," she whispered and then turned to Paul. "Sweetheart, I'm going to have to stitch up the wound." She took the bottle of Steinhager schnapps Hermann handed her. "You know what this tastes like, don't you?"

Paul gave a painful grin. "I have had a drink or two," he admitted.

"Now you can have all you want. It will help dull the pain." She poured the clear liquid into a glass. He took it from her and frowned.

"That much?"

"Yes, that much and more. Drink up, my boy."

He sputtered as he emptied the glass and then another and another. "Stitch away," he said as he lay his head back on the pillow and braced himself. Rosa cleaned the wound, and at the first touch of the needle, Paul slipped into merciful darkness.

Helen checked the clock: 3:00 AM. Deep shadows lined her red, swollen eyes. Ignoring her protests, Hermann had ushered her into the kitchen when Rosa began to stitch up the wound. Helen's face had turned as white as Paul's. Her knees had buckled, and Hermann had caught her with strong arms.

Rosa stepped into the kitchen; her face bathed in perspiration. Tiny rivulets trickled down her glasses, and her blouse was soaking wet. She carried the bowl of water and bloody linen.

"He's going to be fine," she announced.

Helen jumped to her feet and ran into the living room. Paul was asleep. Her eyes welled as she caressed her son's face.

"Careful, do not wake him." Hermann stood behind her. "He's earned some rest. He'll probably sleep for a long time and wake up with a huge hangover."

"He could have been killed." Helen spoke softly.

"Yes, but he's fine now," Hermann said. "He's a brave boy." He patted Helen's arm and left. Back in the kitchen, he found Rosa rummaging through the sacks of food stashed in the corner.

"What're you doing?" He looked at her incredulously.

"I'm going to cook a decent meal," she said.

"At this hour? Why don't you get some sleep and let me do the cooking."

"Do you really think I could sleep a wink?" Rosa said and smiled. "When that boy wakes up, he'll be hungry, and I'm going to serve him the best meal he's had in a long, long time."

Dawn highlighted the new day. Helen had kept vigil at Paul's side. They had weathered another storm and discovered resources they didn't know they had. This time, they were pushed to the limit.

Paul was still asleep. His breath came evenly. His lids fluttered, and he stirred slightly. Helen kissed him softly on the forehead. A tiny tear dropped onto his cheek and rolled down his face.

"You can stop crying now, Mutti. I'm fine," he murmured.

Helen pulled back. Paul's eyes were wide open, and his lips stretched into a grin. He sniffed the air. "I'm starved..."

"Say no more," Rosa said as she entered, carrying a tray with a plate filled with steaming beef stew, hot tea, and three chocolate bars. "I have a cake in the oven. I found flour and sugar. These Americans are quite clever, the way they dehydrate eggs and milk for longtime storage. I've never baked a cake that way, but we shall see."

"I'm sure it'll be delicious." Helen laughed as she helped Paul sit up. She placed a pillow under his injured arm as Rosa set the tray on his lap.

"Do you want me to help you, sweetheart?" Helen asked.

"Mutti, please. I'm not an invalid," Paul said and began to eat with gusto. His discomfort had not affected his appetite. Helen smiled at Rosa, and for one long moment, they clasped hands.

After Paul had finished, he looked at them expectantly.

"I'll get some more." Rosa laughed, took the plate, and hurried into the kitchen, where Hermann sat at the sideboard, listening intently to the radio.

"That boy can eat—"

"Listen to this," he interrupted and turned up the volume.

The announcement was loud and clear, "The Americans forces are repairing some of the bridges and railways to allow supplies to be transported into towns via truck and train within the next few weeks. The new government will be issuing ration stamps to each resident to be exchanged for food, fuel, and various staples. The Allies are doing everything in their power to end the starvation of the German people."

"Do we dare believe what they're saying?" Rosa asked.

"It's high time we got some relief. The war has been over for three months, and our situation has not changed. Like animals, we have to scrape for food. The forest has nearly been stripped bare of anything that would fit inside the pot to be cooked into something. It's a miracle that we have made it this far."

Rosa nodded quietly as her eyes filled up. Hermann pulled her to him; his arms closed around her.

"Yes, I believe what the announcer said to be true. Things will get better. We've hit rock bottom, and now we're on our way up."

Rosa trembled. He lifted her chin, and his eyes searched her face. "It's okay to cry," he said softly.

"But I don't want to cry now." She hastily wiped her eyes. "This is good news."

"Yes, I know, but it's okay to cry."

"Oh, you dear man..." She kissed him tenderly on the mouth and turned to pick up the tray. "Open the door," she said and left the kitchen.

5

The Painting

It was the eyes that gave her a chill. Black and deep-set, they watched from beneath bristly eyebrows as she moved about the room. They reminded her of the ugly wolf in her storybook, who tried to lure the little girl into his trap. A shaggy blob camouflaged most of his upper lip. Her grandfather had a much better-looking mustache, which he fastidiously cleaned and groomed after each meal. Her eyes traveled to the muddy-brown tunic, which contrasted sharply with the clear blue sky in the background. Decorated with colorful military ribbons and insignia, it stretched across his chest and failed to conceal his belly. Anne wondered why her mother kept this dreadful painting on the dining room wall. She had noticed that when she visited her friend Lilli, there was a similar portrait staring from above the wood stove in the living room. The once vibrant colors had taken on a grayish tint, obscuring the man's face as he peered through layers of soot.

Anne recalled the time when two soldiers came to her house. The insignia on the upper sleeve of their black uniforms depicted an odd-shaped black cross against a blood-red background. When she had asked one of the men about it, he told her gruffly that it was a symbol of supremacy and power. She didn't understand the meaning of the words but was afraid to ask further questions. She had noticed by the high pitch of her mother's voice that she was nervous as she led the men into the dining room where the ugly portrait hung. The men saluted the man in the painting and left the room.

"Here's my little red fox." Hermann entered the dining room carrying the game box. "How about a game of chess?"

Anne's face lit up only to turn into a frown. "Let's play in the kitchen," she said. "I don't like this man." She tilted her head sideways toward the painting. Hermann laughed out loud.

"That makes two of us." He placed the game box on the table and walked over to the painting.

He had lost count of the times the SS had showed up at the doorstep and harassed his family because he refused to join their party. The last time they were there, one of them threatened him.

"Mr. Schmidt...for your sake and your family's, you'd better be walking a straight line with that crippled leg of yours, because we're watching you very carefully," the soldier had said sarcastically. "You could make your life a lot easier if you decided to be a loyal German and joined the Fuhrer's party."

Hermann had kept control of his rising anger, and gave them a stiff smile. He said, "Always a pleasure to see you gentlemen." He made a respectful bow, and the SS men burst into malicious laughter and pushed past him.

Helen had released a deep breath and said, "Thanks, Dad. I know how difficult this was for you."

"Don't worry, Helen. They're not going to bother us. I think I've got them convinced that I'm nuts."

Helen stared at him in silence, and he knew what she was thinking. She understood and respected his rejection of the Nazi Party, but she also knew what the SS did with people who refused to be submissive. Several of their neighbors had been arrested for making frivolous remarks, which were taken out of context and reported by Nazi spies. Some of these people never returned.

There was the time when the Gestapo had hammered their door in the middle of the night. Helen was struggling to put on her robe and slippers when she heard shouting. She ran down the hallway and opened the door, only to be pushed aside by two members of the Gestapo, who entered the apartment with their pistols drawn.

"Where is he?" one of them yelled as they searched each room.

"What do you want?" Helen called after them.

They had reached the closed bedroom door at the end of the hallway and kicked it open. It slammed against the wall; things fell to the floor and shattered. The children were asleep. They yanked Paul from his bed, and dragged him away.

Helen panicked, a scream rising in her throat. "Where are you going with my son?"

"He is a traitor."

Hermann appeared from his bedroom. "Leave that boy alone."

"Ah...Mr. Schmidt, it appears the apple doesn't fall far from the tree," one of them said over his shoulder, and they hurried outside. The engine of their Kuebelwagen roared, and they sped away.

"What has my grandson done?" Rosa had joined Helen and Hermann.

"I don't know, but I am going down to the police station to find out." Helen turned and hurried to her bedroom to get dressed.

"I'll go with you," Hermann called after her.

"I don't think that's a good idea," Rosa said. "I will accompany Helen. You take care of the children."

Bessie stood next to Hermann. Her eyes were filled with fear, and she reached for his hand, when they heard Anne calling for her mother.

"It's got to be some kind of mistake," Hermann said and led Bessie back to the children's bedroom.

Dawn crept through the half-open window with a shadowy white quality and began to dispel the darkness. Hermann was slumped against the headboard of Paul's bed, when his head jerked up. He squinted at his watch. It was 6:00 AM. Anne and Bessie had curled up next to him and were sleeping soundly. He tiptoed out of the room. He opened the front door; a brisk wind bit at his cheek. The street looked deserted. He paced the hallway. He clenched his fists as waves of guilt washed over him. He prayed desperately, "Please, God, let my grandson be safe. I'll do anything—join their damn party, whatever it takes—but please don't let them harm him." He was muffling his sobs with his hands, when he heard voices. He opened the apartment door just as Helen, Rosa, and Paul entered the foyer.

"Thank God." He gave Paul a hug.

Helen's eyes were red and swollen. Rosa's flushed cheeks indicated a state of extreme agitation. It was a warning to stay away from her, but he would not today.

"What a nightmare..." Helen paused and raised her head. She turned and walked over to the staircase. Heavy footsteps retreated on the second floor above, and a door slammed.

"That woman doesn't miss anything," Helen said. "Let's go inside."

"I need to get some sleep." Paul yawned and padded back to his room. Hermann noticed that he appeared no worse for the happenings during the night.

Rosa stirred the fire and filled the kettle. "We'll have some tea. The world always looks better after a good cup of tea."

"Was it my fault?" Hermann said. "Are they harassing my grandson because of me?"

"No, Dad. This was all a misunderstanding. It seems that some of Paul's friends had scrawled anti-Nazi graffiti on the remaining wall of Sacred Heart Church." Helen sniffed. "It was harmless, stupid stuff that kids do and should be considered as such. They blew everything out of proportion and kept drilling us nonstop."

"I know their tactics well," Hermann remarked.

"It had happened early in the evening. Paul wasn't even there. He was with us all night. Whoever reported the incident must have thought that Paul took part in it, because he's friends with some of these boys." Helen paused. She looked up at the ceiling.

"The Brenners...do you think it was them? I'm going up there right now and have a talk with that woman." Hermann shot to his feet. Rosa put both hands on his shoulders and pushed him back into his chair.

"Never you mind. We have no proof." The teakettle whistled, and she filled their cups. "We have to let it go and be thankful that the Gestapo finally believed us."

"How is Paul?"

"Dad, you would have been so proud of him. He answered their questions without any sign of fear. His answers were straightforward; they couldn't shake him. I asked him on the way home if he was frightened, and he said that at first he was scared, but he knew he was telling the truth and that was all he could do."

"Opa..." Anne tugged at his arm.

He looked down at her and said, "I think it's time that we rid ourselves of this eyesore." He walked over to the wall and removed the painting. "I've wanted to do this for a long time."

Anne cheered her grandfather. She was clapping her hands when Helen entered the room.

"Dad, what're you doing?" She took the portrait from him.

"Helen, the war is over. We have a new chain of command. There's no reason for us to have to look at his hideous face any longer. We don't have to worry about SS troopers beating down the door to harass us. We hung the picture on the wall because we had no choice, and it kept the Gestapo off our backs. Each time I look at his face, I shudder...what he has done to us; to our country. That man was pure evil."

"What's going on in here?" Paul stuck his head through the door.

"Just in time, my boy. Take this down into the basement and hide it in the farthest corner you can find." Hermann snickered and relieved Helen of the painting. He handed it to Paul.

"Wait a minute." Helen put a restraining hand on Paul's arm. "Do you think it's wise?"

"Certainly. You don't want the Americans to believe that we were Nazi collaborators, like our landlords, the Brenners." He patted her shoulder. "I want you to fetch that beautiful still life that Rosa and I gave you and Fritz for your first wedding anniversary. We'll hang it in its place."

Helen glanced at the outline the painting had left on the wall. Her father was right. There had been a few welcome changes. They no longer feared for their lives every single minute of the day and night. The air attacks had ceased, but there was still confusion all around them. The Americans had promised to create order. Time would tell. Her step was light as she left the room.

"Perfect," Hermann said as he moved back. "This painting brightens up the whole room." He turned to Helen. "Don't you agree? It's like a breath of fresh air. Just think how pleasant our mealtimes will be from now on." He chuckled and winked at Anne as he set up the chessboard.

Helen smiled and returned to the kitchen where she resumed mending the children's clothes. She had patched Anne's pants so many times, the original fabric was difficult to determine. They needed another windfall like the one Hermann had brought home two years earlier. While checking the trap in the forest, he stumbled upon a parachute buried beneath the leaves and quickly bunched it together and headed straight for home. Helen was ecstatic. The parachute measured many yards of tough fabric in a soft coral shade. She and Rosa made pants, shirts, jackets, and dresses for the children. Over Paul's strong objections, that summer, the children were visions in muted coral, easily recognized by everyone.

The sun had disappeared behind the horizon, and dusk crept through the kitchen window. Helen removed her wire-rimmed spectacles and rubbed her eyes. It was time to call it a day.

"Mutti, I've got a job." Paul burst through the door, breathless. She looked up at her tall, handsome son.

"What do you mean...a job?"

"My friend Gerhard works as a dishwasher at the American kitchen. I went with him today and met the mess sergeant, who told me that they need someone to get rid of the garbage and clean the kitchen. So, I'm it."

"American kitchen?" Helen's eyebrows shot up.

"At the Winkler Villa."

Helen frowned. Those beautiful homes up on the hill, which miraculously had been spared by the bombs, and now housed the

75

American officers. The owners were kicked out at moment's notice and forced to seek shelter with relatives and friends. Helen fondly remembered the good times she had while playing rummy with her friends Bertl, Emmy, and Eva. Emmy's house was one of the ones that had been seized, and Helen wondered what had happened to the elegant furnishings and artwork, which took Emmy and her husband years to accumulate.

"The kitchen is just for the officers housed on the hill. They'll pay with food, soap, and stuff." Paul's voice drew Helen back into reality. Her eyes lit up.

"Did you say that they'll give you food?"

"Yes. Here…" He handed her half a loaf of white bread. "They were going to throw it out."

Helen stared at the bread. She couldn't remember the last time she had eaten white bread. What a treat! It would be the highlight of tonight's dinner.

"I have to report at the kitchen every day, and they'll let me know if they have something for me to do," Paul said.

"I don't know…" A gamut of mixed emotions assailed her mind, and she struggled to put things into perspective. It was not long ago that these very people had wreaked death and destruction on the people of Wildenheim, and now they were offering a chance of survival.

Rosa had watched her daughter quietly.

"Helen, don't waste one minute on misguided loyalty to a government that almost destroyed us," she said. "There is a fresh breeze flowing through the country, healthy and strong. We must allow it to get rid of the cobwebs in our minds. It's wonderful that Paul found this job. The food, whatever they give us, will be a welcome addition to our scanty diet."

"You're right," Helen said. Her eyes caressed her son, and she wrapped her arm around him. "I'm so proud of you and how you've taken the initiative to help us."

"Thanks, Mom." Paul wriggled out of her embrace and left the kitchen in a hurry.

Rosa glanced at her daughter. "Helen, you must believe that the Americans will help us rebuild our nation to become a true democracy once more," she said. "War is ugly; war is hell, but as far as the Americans go, I'm with them, and so should you be. We must be realistic. I intend for us to get through this, no matter what we have to do." Rosa turned and vigorously stirred the bubbling concoction in the dented pot.

"I'll get it." Anne ran to answer the doorbell.

"Wait." Helen hurried down the hall. "Don't open that door—"

The words faded as Anne quickly unlocked the door, and was faced with two American soldiers in combat uniforms, rifles slung over their shoulders.

The taller of the two tipped his helmet and spoke to Anne in unintelligible German. Helen observed his rifle and quickly swept Anne up into her arms. "What do you want?" she asked.

The tall man had followed her gaze and said something to the other GI. The second soldier was short and muscular. He pushed his helmet back as his eyes roamed freely over Helen. The tall man frowned and barked a command; the other soldier snapped to attention and stared straight ahead.

"Tell me, what is it you want?" Helen demanded. She struggled to hide her fear. They didn't know that she and Anne were alone in the apartment. Rosa, Hermann, and Bessie had left for their daily jaunt into the forest. She didn't expect them back for hours. Paul was working at the American kitchen.

The tall man smiled kindly and said in English, "We must search your apartment."

Helen shook her head. "I don't know what you're saying. I don't speak your language. Leave us alone. Go away..."

The short soldier scowled and muttered under his breath as he shoved her aside and entered the apartment. The other soldier nodded reassuringly and said slowly in broken German, "It's okay, not to fear." They began their search in the living room where they looked under the sofa, turned Hermann's easy chair over, and left it in that position. They moved quickly through the dining room but took more time rummaging through the hall closet. Helen followed them, carrying Anne in her arms. The tall soldier demanded, "Guns...do you have guns?" He pointed to his rifle. Helen shook her head.

They walked into the master bedroom and pulled out all the dresser drawers. They stopped and stared at the neatly folded underwear, socks, and nightgowns. The shorter man rummaged through her underwear. Helen set Anne on the floor and slammed the drawer shut. "Stay out of my stuff."

The soldiers laughed and continued their search. Helen had regained some of her composure and realized that they did not intend to harm her. They seemed to be looking for weapons. She decided to cooperate more freely and even led them to the secret chamber accessible through the pantry in the kitchen, where in the past, Hermann had hidden his hunting rifles, Helen's and Rosa's jewelry, and other valuables. All those things had long since been removed. The SS had confiscated the rifles, and the other items had been traded for food. When she pointed to the pantry, the soldiers looked at her suspiciously. The short one removed his rifle from his shoulder and cocked it. Helen smiled, brushed past them, and opened the door. The two soldiers peered cautiously through the narrow opening and then squeezed through and entered the tiny chamber. There was barely enough room for them to turn around.

At last, they had finished their search. The tall man turned to Helen and said, "I want to see the cellar." She frowned and shrugged her shoulders. He pointed to the floor. She realized that they wanted to see the basement. She took Anne's hand, stepped in front of them, and motioned them to follow. When she reached the basement, she headed toward their storage room and unlocked the door. She turned and almost bumped into the stocky GI. She looked over his shoulder and searched for the tall one, who had remained at the top of the stairs. She heard him speak on his radio. Fear crept up her spine.

Anne shivered as she raised her eyes fearfully to Helen. "Mutti, I'm scared; let's go back upstairs."

"It's all right, sweetheart. We'll only be a minute."

The GI glanced at the bare shelves and poked around the empty coal bin and wire potato crate. He moved an old water barrel and stepped back. He snorted his disapproval as Adolf Hitler's piercing eyes stared at him through a veil of cobwebs and with one well-aimed kick, eliminated the Fuhrer's stern countenance. He looked at Helen who shrugged and said crisply, "I didn't like him either."

The soldier approached her and studied her face closely. He placed his hand around her neck and pulled her close. She resisted and pushed against him with her hands. He tightened his grip and forced his mouth on hers. Anne began to sob, and the soldier pulled away from Helen. He directed his head toward the door. "Go away...now." His voice was hoarse. Helen let out a scream and he clamped his hand across her mouth and shoved her against the wall. Her mind reeled. He was strong, and she knew that her struggles were useless. All she could think was that Anne must never be a witness to what was certainly going to happen.

"Anne, go upstairs...please..." she begged.

"Don't hurt Mutti," Anne cried and yanked his arm. His vicious kick landed in midair when Anne ducked away and began screaming hysterically.

Two strong hands wrapped around the GI's neck, and pulled him away. Helen sank into the wall. The tall soldier bellowed at the other man and sent him upstairs. He then turned to Helen and spoke in a soft, apologetic voice. He looked at Anne, who clung to her mother's skirt, and he reached out to touch her hair. Anne cringed. He pointed at his chest and said in broken German, "I have daughter...with red hair..." He pointed at Anne's fuzzy hair. He squatted down, but Anne refused to look at him. "You're a brave girl."

Helen stared blankly as he tipped his helmet and left.

"Mutti, they're bad soldiers," Anne whispered.

Helen glanced at her daughter for a moment and said, "Sweetheart, these men had no intention of hurting us."

Anne looked at her skeptically as Helen struggled for the proper words. "They were just making a joke. You know, like when we play hide-and-seek and Paul jumps out from behind a tree making faces and scaring us?" Anne nodded slowly. "Let's just forget about the whole incident. We don't need to tell anyone about this." Anne stared at her mother in silence, and Helen suggested, "Let's go upstairs and share that last piece of apple strudel. What do you say?" Anne's face dissolved into a smile, and she eagerly took Helen's hand and dragged her forward. On their way up the stairs, they bumped into Mary Stringer.

"Helen, what in the world...?"

"Anne, please go upstairs. I want to speak with Mary for a few minutes. Help yourself to the strudel. Go ahead."

"I'll save you some." Anne ran up the steps.

"Helen…" Mary stared at Helen's disheveled appearance.

"Oh, Mary…" Helen burst into tears.

Mary wrapped her arm around her as they sat down on the steps. "I saw the two soldiers. They searched our apartment too. Dad took them into the cellar. Then they knocked on the Brenners' door. I guess you were last on the list. I didn't know that you were home alone; I would have sent Dad down to be with you." She pulled out a handkerchief and wiped Helen's face. "Did they hurt you?"

Helen took the hankie and blew her nose. "Only one of them. He tried to hurt me, but Anne kicked him and screamed; then the other soldier came running. He got very angry and yelled and sent him away and then spoke to me in English. By the tone of his voice, I gathered that it was an apology. I'm not sure; I couldn't understand him."

"How horrible!" Mary was incensed. "What about Anne?"

"I tried to convince her that it was just a game. I don't want my family to know about this."

"He should be reported!" Mary cried.

"Reported? Where and to whom?" Helen said. "We have no police force, and the Americans are in charge. I'm sure they will take up for their own. We've just lost the war and have no rights." Helen sniffed. "Besides, I wasn't hurt, just frightened."

The two women walked slowly up the stairs.

"Hmm, something smells good." Paul walked into the kitchen. He lifted the lid and peered into the battered saucepan. "What's cooking?"

"Wait and see." Bessie slapped his hand and pushed him away.

"Don't tell me you're cooking again?" Paul winked at Rosa who was slicing mushrooms.

"Your sister has a real talent. You've eaten her cooking more times than you know," Rosa said with a chuckle.

"It's beef stew, stupid. Can't you tell?" Bessie snickered.

"I don't see any meat."

Bessie dismissed the remark with a haughty snort, and he laughed as he stuck a small package wrapped in brown paper into her face. She yanked it out of his hands and spread it out on the table. Rosa peered over her spectacles. The beef bones in front of her still had enough meat on them to make their meal a real beef stew. The bones were quickly dropped into the pot, and neither Bessie nor Rosa questioned how he got them.

"Did I hear a vehicle in the driveway?" Helen peeked through the door. She carried a wicker laundry basket filled with clothes taken from the line.

"I got a ride home today," Paul said.

Rosa raised her head. "Who do we know that still has a car?"

"When I left the kitchen today, I got a ride from one of the soldiers." Paul hesitated. "It was strange. When we pulled into the driveway, he asked me if I had a little sister with red hair."

"That's an odd question," Helen said. "What did you tell him?"

"I just nodded."

"What's his name?"

"Jim."

"What's he look like?" Helen asked and held her breath.

Paul shrugged. "Like a soldier. Why do you ask?"

"Never mind." Helen busied herself folding the sheets.

The next day, Paul came home with a cardboard box filled with treasures. The whole family gazed in amazement as he pulled out each precious item. There was a carton of dried milk, a box of instant egg yolks, three loaves of white bread, a tin of processed meat, a bag of coffee beans, a large bar of soap, and a pack of cigarettes. Rosa was speechless. Helen cradled the small bag to her chest.

"Look, Dad, real coffee!" She danced around the kitchen. "This is like Christmas!"

Hermann quickly reached for the cigarettes. "They're not cigars, but they'll do."

"Jim gave me all this stuff," Paul said. "He told me it's for you. He also asked if you would be willing to do his laundry in exchange for food."

Helen shrank back in horror.

"You tell him that we'll be happy to do his laundry as long as he keeps the food coming," Rosa said firmly. She glanced at Helen, who had remained silent. "Helen, what's the matter with you?"

"I'll do his laundry, but you'll take it to him. I don't want him coming here," Helen said emphatically. Rosa and Paul stared at her as she jumped up and left the kitchen, slamming the door behind her.

From that day on, thanks to Jim, they went to bed at night with their bellies full. Helen and Rosa even shared some of the food with the Stringers.

"Dad, what are you reading?"

Hermann looked up and folded the flimsy four-page newspaper. "It's the slimmed down version of the *Spessart Echo.* A far cry from the newspaper Karl used to publish before his printing shop was blown to bits. Listen to this." He began to read, "It says here that the Americans are clearing the roads and have repaired much of the damaged railroad tracks, which means that food and fuel supplies will start rolling into Wildenheim regularly."

"Do we dare hope, Dad? Is the worst over?" Helen's eyes clung to his face.

"Who knows? It says here that CARE, an American organization, has already begun shipping packages with food supplies into war-torn countries." He looked at her and chuckled. "Maybe you'll be able to stop doing the American's laundry soon." He read on silently.

Helen walked up to the window. *Not a minute too soon,* she thought. Touching that man's clothes was humiliating and made her gag.

"The Americans are rebuilding the bridge across the Main River." Hermann looked up. "Once we're able to cross the river again, we'll look up Fritz's parents...if they're still alive."

"The Americans are not doing this for us!" Helen exclaimed furiously. "They're repairing the bridge because they need to use it." Hermann stared at his daughter and put down the newspaper.

"Sit down," he said. "I've been meaning to talk to you." He took her hand; his voice was soft and low. "I sense a lot of hostility; you never miss a chance to denigrate the American troops." Helen opened her mouth to speak, but he shook his head. "No, let me finish. This hatred will eat you up alive and spread to your children, who are very tuned into you. Remember, the war has forced us to live together in such proximity that we learned to read each other's thoughts. Your children will grow up in a world that has survived a collision of nations who have consequently come together and forged a peace. Our enemies are now our allies, and all animosity must be pushed aside. This is the only way."

Helen violently shook her head, but he kept on talking, "So, we start over; we've done it before, and we must accept the hand that reaches out to us, no matter what nationality. We're lucky to be alive, and you've had a huge part in that. This family looks up to you. You are the pillar; you're our inspiration, and you have set an example of fierce determination and unquestionable courage. I am terribly proud of you and love you so much."

Tears streamed down Helen's cheeks, and she dropped her head onto the table. He gathered her into his arms. She cried for a long time, and he rocked her as he used to when she was a little girl. Finally, he whispered into her ear, "Reason is our soul's left hand; faith her right."

Helen looked up and smiled through her tears. He gently wiped her cheeks with his hand. "Remember when I used to tell you that?"

"Yes, I remember it very well. John Donne packed much wisdom into these few words. Thanks, Dad, I needed to hear that." She took a deep breath, and a surge of energy rushed through her veins. Her body felt light and airy, like a feather that drifts in the breeze. She looked at her father's face, those gentle gray eyes that clung to hers sternly, but lovingly, and then he winked at her. She laughed through her tears. "Don't worry, Dad; I'm going to be just fine."

"That's my girl." He hugged her to him.

Helen was tending her vegetable garden. There would be a good crop this season. The green beans, lettuce, and cabbage were thriving; even the crippled peach tree was loaded with fruit.

"Mutti, Jim's here." Anne came running, followed by a tall soldier in uniform. Helen recognized him as one of the two men who had come to search her home.

"Hello." He stopped in front of her. Recognition quickened in her expression, and she gasped. Each time she had done his laundry, she had cursed the wrong man.

"Mutti, I think he wants his clothes." Anne looked at her mother, who was acting strangely.

The soldier began to speak in a mix of German and English. When she didn't reply, he pulled a small dictionary from his pocket and pointed with his finger. Helen stepped closer. She understood. He was leaving, being transferred back to the United States. She nodded, and he reached into his breast pocket and pulled out a picture of his wife and child, a little girl about the same age as Anne. He said proudly in German, "My daughter...red hair...like hers." He smiled and pointed at Anne's hair. Anne was munching on the chocolate bar he had brought her. Her little heart-shaped mouth was framed by a light brown chocolate mustache.

"Let's go into the house and wash you off." Helen took Anne's sticky little hand. "I'll get your laundry." She motioned for him to follow.

Helen handed him the package and saw him out the door. He paused and said, "*Vielen Dank...*" He watched her face intently and made a step forward, and then hesitated.

Helen smiled and gave him a hug. "Good-bye, Jim, and God-speed," she said.

Helen glanced out the kitchen window. The color of the sun had deepened to magenta, and the sky was streaked in magnificent yellow, orange, and crimson. Wreaths of smoke rose from the back-yard. She spotted Mr. Stringer walking up the path.

"What's up?" she called out the window.

"We're having a bonfire. Come join us."

"You're wasting wood," Helen cautioned.

"Not at all," he said and grinned. "We're burning his paintings. Go get yours."

A fitting demise, Helen mused. Too bad he had escaped such a well-deserved fate in real life. There were millions of people who would have liked to see him roast. She rushed down the basement steps and retrieved the dilapidated canvas. She looked at it and laughed hysterically. The tattered pieces of his faceless image quivered as she ran up the stairway where she was joined by her family. They hurried into the backyard. Several of their neighbors had gathered around the pyre; others were still arriving and flinging their paintings into the flames. Mary Stringer served weak coffee in china cups. Lilli's mother had brought her harmonica and played a lively tune accompanied by the rhythmic clapping of hands.

The fire matched the colors of the sky. Tiny sparks took to the air and the flames grew higher. The group watched as the fire gave off warmth that filled their hearts with hope. The healing process had begun.

On the second floor, behind the curtain in her kitchen window, Mrs. Brenner screwed her mouth up in disapproval of the scene below her. She turned and plodded into the living room where her husband poured precious brandy into two snifters. They smiled at each other and then turned and raised their glasses to the man in the painting, who stared at them with indifference.

6

The Colonel

The colonel wants to rent Hermann's Ruhe."

The ball of yarn dropped from Helen's hand and meandered toward Rosa, who reached for it as it passed her feet. "You must be joking," Helen said.

"I'm serious, Mutti. I don't know how the colonel found out about Hermann's Ruhe, but he approached me at the kitchen today and inquired if it is available for rent. I told him that I would ask you. He said he would probably only stay a few months, until he gets his orders to go home."

Rosa glanced sideways at her daughter, who had resumed knitting Anne's sweater with a furrowed brow, her lips tightly pressed together, and mentioned casually, "We could certainly use the money."

Helen didn't answer. Waves of anger washed over her, and a conflict of emotions raged within her. During these past years, she had been forced to swallow her pride countless times only to be haunted by shame afterward. Hermann's Ruhe had been desecrated once already. Now a stranger, who not long ago was their archenemy, wants to stay there, sleep in their beds, sit at their table, and walk in the beautiful garden. She lay down her knitting, rose abruptly, and walked over to the window. There was a long period of silence before she turned and said, "I'm totally against renting Hermann's Ruhe to anyone, least of all to an American."

"What's going on here?" Hermann entered the room. "I heard you talking about Hermann's Ruhe—"

"Dad, we need to make a decision here, and I think you're the one to make it," Helen interrupted in a fuss. She walked over to the couch and sat down. "Paul, go ahead, tell your grandfather the whole story."

"An American colonel is interested in renting Hermann's Ruhe," Paul began.

Hermann's jaw dropped. "How did he find out about our cottage?"

"I'm not sure. I was telling the cook the story about the time we had to flee from there, chased by bullets. Cook is friends with the colonel. He may have mentioned it to him. Anyway, the colonel wants to meet us at Hermann's Ruhe this coming Saturday so that he can look the place over."

Helen bristled with indignation. "He does? He's taking a lot for granted, isn't he?" she said.

Hermann fixed his wife and daughter with a steady stare. Hermann's Ruhe was their sanctuary, a place filled with precious memories. He was certain how Rosa felt about the matter; he knew where his daughter stood, and he was inclined to agree with her, but they had to be practical. The income would help make their life a little easier.

"If you want my opinion, the extra income would be worth having to turn Hermann's Ruhe over to a total stranger for a few months," Rosa said. "There are so many things we desperately need."

Hermann cleared his throat. "I guess it wouldn't hurt to talk to the colonel." He turned to Paul. "Tell him to meet us on Saturday at two o'clock. Does he know how to get there?"

"I'll give him directions." Paul ran out the door, leaving behind a deep silence as the three people contemplated this latest development.

"He may not want to rent the cottage. After all, there's no electricity, and there's no running water…" Hermann's voice drifted off. When his wife and daughter remained silent, he rose and left the room.

They arrived at Hermann's Ruhe at one o'clock on Saturday. Rosa believed in being early for any appointment. It was a glorious day. The early fall sunshine warmed their faces. They opened all the windows, and Bessie and Anne immediately grabbed the chess game and headed for the gazebo.

"We might as well occupy our time while we're waiting for the man. Paul, get the scythe; this grass needs cutting." Hermann handed Paul the key for the shed.

Helen walked through the rooms with a critical eye. She wondered if the American realized how isolated Hermann's Ruhe was; it occurred to her that they must establish rules. She ran out to her father who put down the scythe and wiped his brow.

"Dad, if he decides to rent the cottage, we must make sure he understands what we expect of him. Rent must be paid on time; the place is to be kept clean; if he breaks anything—" She ticked off the items on her fingers.

"I know," Hermann interrupted. "I have already thought about all that. Let's see what happens. We may not like him and decide against letting him move in."

Exactly at two o'clock, a jeep pulled into the small grass plot above the fence. The colonel advanced with a brisk gait, sending showers of stones cascading down the hill. Hermann dropped his scythe and hurried to meet him.

Everyone's eyes were on the colonel as he strode through the open gate. Tall and broad shouldered, he wore a full dress uniform. His face, shaded by the visor of his hat, was tanned and clean-shaven. Helen had left the porch and joined Hermann while Rosa watched from the kitchen window. Helen's eyes swept over the man, and she had to admit he represented a striking figure of near perfection; however, she attributed most of his handsome appearance to the elegant uniform he wore. He stopped in front of them, clicked his heels, removed his hat, and stretched out his hand to Hermann. "Anthony Blake, *sehr angenehm*," he said in heavily accented German.

"Hermann Schmidt," Hermann said and turned to Helen, who had already extended her hand. "This is my daughter, Helen."

The colonel bowed his head and brushed her hand with his lips. "Ma'am." He raised his head, and their eyes met briefly. He had a strong face with a prominent nose. Thick lashes extended across his eyes, which were a light brown shade laced with amber specks that reminded her of fall when nature put on its most beautiful colors and had a final fling before the long winter sleep. The colonel exuded confidence and refinement and was not at all what she had expected.

They turned, and Hermann led the way to the cottage. The colonel stepped back to allow Helen to walk in front of him. She was aware that he was observing her and tugged at her ragged skirt and cotton blouse. She ran her fingers through her hair. She hadn't been to a beauty shop in years, as she and Rosa had become experts by necessity at cutting everyone's hair.

They stopped beneath the plaque. The colonel studied it at length and then pointed to Hermann and smiled, his teeth gleaming white.

"My son-in-law and his father and I built Hermann's Ruhe," Hermann said proudly. The colonel slowly nodded his head and walked up the porch. His eyes lit up as he studied the breathtaking view. He paused and inhaled deeply.

"Magnificent," he murmured.

Hermann pointed a quizzical glance at Helen, who shrugged her shoulders. The colonel turned and stepped inside the cottage.

Rosa had been watching through the door and quickly busied herself in the kitchen.

"Colonel Blake, this is my wife, Rosa."

The colonel took her hand and kissed it. Rosa blushed furiously, and she smiled shyly.

"Come, I'll show you around," Hermann said and led the colonel into the living room.

"What do you think?" Helen whispered to Rosa.

"Let's go outside." Rosa grabbed the water bucket, and they walked over to the well. "I know one thing; he's a gentleman, and a handsome one at that, even though he is an American," she said with a giggle.

"Mother, you're incorrigible. Seriously...he seems like a nice man." Helen chewed on her lower lip. "I must admit, when he kissed my hand, it made me feel like a woman for the first time in a long time." She paused, and her eyes welled. "I miss Fritz so much, and I get panicky at the thought of never seeing him again." Rosa dropped the bucket and pulled her close.

"I know, dear, but you must be strong and keep believing, and one of these days he'll walk through the door and surprise all of us."

"I hope you're right." Helen brushed her hand across her eyes.

At that moment, Hermann and the colonel stepped out onto the porch and walked toward the back of the yard. They approached the gazebo where they were greeted by angry voices.

"Girls, mind your manners. We have company," Hermann said. He pointed at the colonel. "Meet Colonel Blake; he's considering renting our cottage." He turned to the colonel. "These are my granddaughters, Bessie and Anne." The girls jumped up, curtsied, and stared at him with their mouths open as their eyes hung curiously on the colorful insignia decorating his coat.

"Hello, children." The colonel smiled and stepped up to get a closer look at the chessboard. "Who is next?" he asked in broken German.

"It's my turn," Anne exclaimed, "and Bessie will not give me time to think." The colonel glanced at the chessboard and moved Anne's white pawn to take Bessie's black one, allowing the white queen to check the black king.

"Checkmate," the colonel declared.

Anne released a triumphant cry and jumped into the air. The colonel noticed that Bessie's eyes had filled with tears and added quickly, "I challenge you." He pointed at her and then touched his chest. Bessie's eyes lit up, and she nodded emphatically. The colonel swung his long legs across the wooden bench vacated by Anne, who had joined her grandfather. The game began. Hermann took Anne by the hand, and they left.

"What's he doing?" Helen asked when they stepped up onto the porch.

"He's challenged Bessie to a game of chess."

"What?"

"He seems to be enjoying himself."

They entered the living room and sat around the table. "What did he say?" Rosa asked.

"About what?" Hermann grinned mischievously.

Rosa playfully slapped his arm. "Does he like our cottage?"

"Well, he seems impressed. He was a little shocked to discover that we do not have any electricity, although the fact that there's no running water didn't seem to bother him. As far as I understood him, he said that fighting a war and all, he was used to getting by without running water."

"Did you mention the rent we agreed upon?"

"Two hundred marks a month is fine with him. He will rent on a monthly basis, as he expects orders at any time to return to America."

"Dad, I'm amazed how the two of you came to an agreement in spite of the language barrier. I'm proud of you." Helen squeezed his arm.

"He said that he wants us to feel free to come up any time and take care of the grass, harvest the fruit, etc., and, of course, attend to Rosa's flower garden."

Bessie's laughter rang loudly as she and the colonel strolled through the grass. Bessie skipped up the porch steps.

"Mutti, I won! I won!" Bessie's cheeks were flushed, and her eyes glittered as the colonel watched her out of the corner of his eye, amused. "The colonel showed me some great moves. Watch out, Opa and Anne, next time we play, I'm going to crush you."

"Oh yeah?" Anne took one threatening step forward, and Bessie shrieked and fled with Anne in hot pursuit.

Rosa offered the colonel a cup of tea, which he politely declined, pointing at his watch. He nodded at the women, and Hermann accompanied him to the gate. The colonel walked with a deliberately slow gait to allow Hermann to keep up with him.

Helen had watched the two men and said to Rosa, "What a kind and thoughtful man. He almost makes me want to forget that he is our enemy."

"You cannot view him in that light and take his money," Rosa said.

"Oh yes, I can. Just watch me."

Rosa clicked her tongue. "I don't know about you sometimes. You have gotten very hard."

"The war changed all of us," Helen said pensively and then put her arm around Rosa. "Let's make plans on how we're going to spend the money."

"That will not be difficult, my dear." Rosa released a happy sigh. There were so many things they needed. She glanced briefly at her old plaid skirt. There was a time when she would never have worn it outside the house. Now it was resurrected and constituted one of her better garments. She chuckled as Helen looked at her expectantly. "Well," Rosa began, "we may want to stock up on coal and fill the potato bin, buy shoes for the children and maybe for us too. Maybe we can purchase at least one bicycle or even two. The hike up to the lodge is getting to be a bit much for me."

Helen laughed heartily. "Mother, just think, for the first time, we're making plans for the future. Isn't it exciting?" She took Rosa by the hand and twirled her around.

"I see you have started the party already." Hermann had joined them. "I brought something to help us celebrate in style." He whisked out a small flask of Steinhager and passed it to Rosa.

"Don't mind if I do," she said and took a swig, and then she handed the flask to Helen who raised it to her lips.

"What about us?" Bessie and Anne had approached looking at them expectantly.

Helen sputtered as the strong, dry spirit cooled her throat. "I don't think so." She laughed and handed the flask back to Hermann. "Come along, girls, we have something for you that's much more appropriate. Your grandmother has baked blueberry muffins, which we brought along." The girls screamed with delight and dragged their mother up the porch steps.

The colonel climbed into his jeep. The splendid panorama of Wildenheim unfolded in the valley below. The swell of the hills, the touches of gold and red that announced the change of the season, were a poignant reminder of his home in America. It seemed an eternity ago that he had hiked the Blue Ridge Mountains of Virginia with his family. The world was different then. He closed his eyes to the vivid image of his two daughters. How they must have grown since he last saw them. The girls were beautiful, like their mother, Katie, who dutifully wrote him every month. Her letters were cold and impersonal, as they gave an account of the girls' activities only. He could not bring himself to write back. He and Katie had drifted apart long before he landed on the beaches in France.

He had always been discreet, and his liaisons never meant anything to him. The long absences from home with the military provided many opportunities, and he felt justified in seizing them. He wasn't sure how she had found out, but when she confronted him, he just shrugged it off, gathered her into his arms, and vowed that she was the only real love in his life. She pushed him away, angry. She denounced him bitterly, and he resented it, for he believed himself to be a loving husband and father. He found excuses to stay away from home as he nursed his injured pride.

He lit a cigarette and inhaled deeply. Thoughts about Katie filled him with a deep longing, and he knew that he still cared for her. He should have died on Omaha Beach. His men had dropped like flies all around him. The screams of the wounded still rang in his ears. The coastline was littered with the dead. Something happened to him that day that changed his life forever. The war had wreaked havoc with the prevailing aspects of his mind and forced him to question his behavior. He was haunted by remorse for the pain he had caused his family, and he believed that once he returned from the war, Katie would ask him for a divorce.

The colonel started the engine. Children's voices rose through the orchard. They were picking apples. He raised his head, and his eyes narrowed. The German woman piqued his interest. She was beautiful and carried herself with pride and dignity in the face of the most punishing circumstances. He had sensed a subtle hostility and decided that it was not necessarily directed at him but at what he represented. He wondered about her husband. He might not even be alive, and yet she persevered, hoping against hope that he would return to her. He was moved by what he had learned about this family today and respected their courage in dealing with reality. He shifted into gear and drove off.

Hermann locked the front door. He leaned on his cane and surveyed the property with a sweeping glance.

"Everything looks okay. The house is spotless, and the grass is cut. The colonel can move in tomorrow." He turned and limped down the steps. Paul, Bessie and Anne were already waiting at the gate. He looked over his shoulder. "Ladies, let's go."

Helen and Rosa lingered on the porch as they inhaled the spectacular sunset. "We won't be able to witness the beautiful view from here for a while." Rosa sighed.

"We'll be back to take care of the gardens and the lawn. I'm sure the colonel won't mind if you come up to the porch and sneak a peek," Hermann said as his wife and daughter met up with him. "He did mention to me that he was interested in going hunting, and I had to explain to him about our laws, which seem to be much stricter than in America. I showed him my hunting license. He was surprised to learn that it requires a written and practical exam to earn a license, and that I was assigned a certain area where I'm allowed to hunt."

They took the shortcut down the hill, which Hermann navigated carefully with the help of his wolf's head cane. They crossed the little stream and saw the smoke coming from the Gypsy cave.

"I didn't know the Gypsies had returned," Rosa said to Hermann.

"I thought we were rid of them for good," Hermann growled. They heard women's laughter, and a man appeared from the depths of the cave. He was of medium height, with long, stringy hair and a shaggy beard. He stared at Anne with dark, piercing eyes. Helen reached for Anne's hand and held it tightly.

"Beautiful child," the man said. His eyes never left Anne's face. "Beautiful hair." He pointed at Anne's red curls.

"You mind your own business. Stay away from us," Hermann snarled, and they hurried on.

"The colonel wants to talk you." Paul had returned from kitchen duty bringing the aroma of fried chicken with him. Helen tensed. It had been three weeks since the colonel had moved into Hermann's Ruhe. They had planned to cut the grass and weed the gardens within the next couple of days.

"Is something wrong? Has he received new orders?"

"I don't think so. He just wants to ask you a question. I don't know what it's all about; I'm just the messenger. He'll stop by later on today." Paul left the room.

"You better hang around to help with the translation," Helen called after him.

She was staring out the kitchen window, wondering what the colonel had on his mind, when the doorbell rang. She listened as Paul answered the door. It was the colonel all right; she could hear his soft drawl. She rose and stepped into the hallway. The colonel was charming as usual as he greeted her. She invited him into the living room, where they found Hermann dozing in his favorite chair. The book he was reading had slipped to the floor.

"Dad," she said as she gently shook his arm. "Colonel Blake is here."

Hermann opened his eyes and smiled. He stretched out his hand. "Colonel Blake, it's nice to see you. Please have a seat." The colonel took the chair next to the sofa. "How do you like living at Hermann's Ruhe? Is everything to your satisfaction?" Hermann asked just as Paul entered to join them.

"No problems at all. I must say you could not have picked a more beautiful spot for your cottage. As matter of fact, I haven't experienced anything like it since I left my country, but…there is one thing missing."

Hermann leaned forward and listened intently as the colonel continued, "You need electricity."

"I heartily agree." Hermann nodded emphatically. "When we began construction, we knew that due to its remote location, Hermann's Ruhe would not have power for a while. Then the war came. We're hoping that somewhere down the line, when order is once more restored and we'll be able to get on our feet again…" The words hung in the air.

The colonel addressed Paul in English.

"The colonel is going to have wires run up to Hermann's Ruhe from the Spessart Hof. He has checked on all the details, and it could be done within a couple of days," Paul translated.

He had to repeat the words before they registered with Hermann and Helen. Hermann's eyebrows shot up, and he opened his mouth to speak when the colonel turned to Paul. "Tell him there will be no charge," he said. "It will be my pleasure to do this for your family."

Helen's hand flew to her face as she stared at the colonel. Electricity meant they could use a stove, play the radio, stay up way beyond dark, and not spoil their eyesight with the kerosene lamps.

She was marveling at all the comforts electricity would bring when she heard Hermann say, "The answer is yes, yes." Hermann's smile was incredulous. "If you could do that for us, we would be forever in your debt, and the least we can do is waive the rent while you live at Hermann's Ruhe."

The colonel motioned to Paul that he understood and said, "I am afraid I must insist on paying as we had agreed." He rose, smiled, and nodded. Helen walked him to the door.

Hermann came into the kitchen and rested his cane against the wall. "It's raw and chilly today. Cold weather's moving in; I can feel it in my bones." He rubbed his hands as he stood in front of the stove. He hummed quietly, glancing sideways at Helen. His face stretched into a huge grin.

"It's fall, Dad," she said and continued reading the newspaper. Finally, she folded the paper and looked up. "I don't dread the cold weather as I did last year. Finally, we have some money to buy coal..." She paused when she noticed he was smiling broadly. "What's the matter?"

Hermann cocked his forefinger and whispered, "Follow me. There's something I want to show you."

Helen jumped to her feet, and they left the apartment. They descended the front steps. Her eyes fell on two battered bicycles leaning against the iron railing. She stood still midway and gasped. "Are these ours? Is this what you did this morning when you disappeared on us?"

Helen skipped down the remaining steps and stared at the bikes. Her eyes searched his face. "Dad, you didn't steal these?"

"Yes, they're ours, and, no, I didn't steal them. I bought them on the black market with the rent money we got from the colonel."

Helen was speechless.

"Well, say something. I know they're not showpieces, but they're functional, and we can spruce them up a bit."

"Dad, they're beautiful." Helen threw her arms around him. "I know that you must have searched long and hard to find these. We better bring them into the apartment right now, before they disappear." She lifted one of the bicycles and proceeded to carry it up the steps.

"Wait, don't you want to give it a spin first? I know the tires aren't the best…"

Helen put down the bike, swung her leg across the seat, and rode down the long driveway. Her cheeks were flushed as she raised her arms and peddled fast. She turned, sat on the handlebars, and rode facing backward.

Hermann laughed heartily. "It looks like you haven't forgotten anything."

Helen stopped the bike in front of him. Her breath came in strong gusts. "This felt so good!" she exclaimed. "I can't wait to show the bikes to the children. They're going to be thrilled."

"Mutti, the colonel wants you to come up to Hermann's Ruhe and check out the electricity." Paul carried the large coral tote bag filled with kindling as he followed Rosa and Bessie, who had just returned from the forest. Rosa took the bag from Paul and transferred the kindling to the large basket next to the stove.

Helen kept stirring the bubbling rabbit stew. She bit her lips to keep them from twitching into a smile. She was quivering inside but managed to ask calmly, "Has anyone noticed anything in the hallway?"

Bessie and Paul dashed through the kitchen door at the same time; they collided, and each tried the keep the other from being first. Their struggle came to an abrupt end, when Rosa placed her hands firmly on their shoulders.

"Excuse me, children," she said calmly as she stepped in front of them. "Well, what do we have here?"

Paul and Bessie gathered around her. Helen heard their gasps as she leaned against the kitchen doorframe, her arms crossed in front of her. Her eyes filmed over as she watched her family admire the newly acquired treasures.

They decided to take the shortcut, and when they passed the cave one of the Gypsies emerged, and scrutinized their bicycles with greedy eyes. The polished chrome sparkled in the afternoon sun. Hermann had painted the fenders black, and Rosa covered the seats with the trusty old standby, the coral parachute fabric that Hermann had found in the forest so long ago. Hermann rode one bike with Bessie on the backseat and Helen the other with Anne, who held on tightly to her mother.

They had reached the little stream in less than an hour. They got off their bikes, crossed over, and walked the steep, rocky path that led up to Hermann's Ruhe. The colonel's jeep was parked on the grassy pad on top of the hill. As they approached the gate, Hermann stopped and examined the wires leading from the tall pole in the parking lot to the cottage.

Helen watched her father; she knew what he was thinking. He caught her eyes.

"What a beautiful sight." His voice caught.

Helen nodded emphatically. Good things had happened lately. They had much to be grateful for. If only Fritz would come home. There still had been no word from him. The newspaper announced that Russia held many German soldiers imprisoned, and the Allies were negotiating their release. It gave her new reason for hope.

They were pushing the bikes through the gate when they heard a woman's laughter. Hermann stared blankly at Helen and she just shrugged. Smoke rose from the chimney. The early October sun was riding near the zenith, and fluffy cloudlets rolled across the sky. The colonel stood on the porch wearing blue jeans and a beige sweater. He waved as he descended the steps. It was the first time they had seen him in civilian clothes. Anne broke away from her mother and ran toward him. He lifted her up high and swung her around as she shrieked with pleasure.

"Hello." The colonel smiled and stretched out his hand. Helen was always amazed at the firmness of his handshake. They leaned the bikes against the house, and he invited them inside. The enticing aroma of freshly baked bread assailed their senses. A tall, slender woman in her mid-twenties stood in the kitchen, wearing a bright yellow apron over a wool skirt and white sweater. Her blond hair draped down to her shoulders. *A perfect frame to complement a perfect picture,* Helen thought. The beauty of her face was accented by deep blue eyes.

"Please meet my friend Anneliese," the colonel said. Hermann's mouth dropped, and Helen nudged him gently with her elbow as she reached for her hand.

The colonel was eager to take them on a tour through the cottage. He pointed to the ceiling light in the kitchen. It was covered with a blue and white fabric shade. Wall switches and outlets had been placed in all of the rooms. He flicked the switch and left his landlords in awe as they stared at the light. The colonel grinned and led them to the rear of the cottage. There were ceiling lights in the living room and bedrooms; even the outside bathroom had a wall light, which dispersed all the eerie shadows that terrorized Anne.

"Let's have some refreshment," Anneliese said. She removed a pound cake glazed with chocolate frosting from the table next to the tiny electric oven that Hermann had bought years ago. The colonel had retrieved it from the basement where it had been stored until they would be able to use it. Helen inhaled the fragrant scent as she sipped the coffee slowly. This was genuine coffee, none of the ersatz stuff that was available to them at exorbitant prices.

Anne and Bessie couldn't get enough of the cake. Anne had licked the icing before she devoured the cake. When they were finished, the girls asked if they could pick blackberries. "I think the blackberry season is over," Hermann said, but the girls begged until he gave in.

"Don't go too far. We'll be leaving shortly. We'll call you when we're ready."

Anneliese brought two small wicker baskets from the kitchen, and Anne and Bessie ran out the door.

The colonel invited Hermann to smoke a cigar, and they stepped outside. Helen helped Anneliese clear the table. She grabbed the milk can to fetch water from the well.

"I'll do it."

"I don't mind." Helen slipped out the door.

Anneliese stared after her. Wildenheim was a small town. She had heard of the Schmidt family, who used to own a wholesale textile business in town, which had been destroyed during one of the early air attacks. Suddenly, she felt terribly ashamed. Tears welled in her eyes. She turned quickly when Helen returned. She filled the kettle and put it on the stove. Anneliese was silent for a long time, and then she said, "I'm sure you must think—"

"I don't think anything," Helen interrupted and then quickly added, "I want you to give me the recipe for the cake glaze. It's delicious. The girls loved it."

"It's simple…but the ingredients…" Anneliese paused.

"Yes, I know. We can't get them now, but there will be a time when we can," Helen said firmly.

"You know he is married," Anneliese whispered, and before Helen could answer, she said, "He says he loves me, but we don't talk about a future together. He'll go back to his country when the time comes." She looked at Helen. "Please don't think badly of me…"

Helen quickly stepped forward and put her arms around the girl. "I'm in no way qualified to pass judgment on anyone, trust me. If you knew, you would never believe some of the things I've done." She gently wiped the tears from Anneliese's face and lifted up her chin. "Can we be friends?"

"I'd like that," Anneliese said with a smile.

Hermann and the colonel passed the kitchen window in a cloud of smoke. Their conversation was animated and laced with laughter. "Your father and Tony don't appear to have any language difficulties," Anneliese remarked.

Helen nodded and said, "I'm amazed how well they're conversing. My son has a job at the American kitchen. He's picking up the English language fast…" She paused and her eyes widened. She ran to the window and spotted Bessie tearing down the path, screaming, "Mutti. Mutti." Bessie stumbled and fell, immediately got up, and kept running.

"Anne's gone!" she cried over and over again. Helen froze as Anneliese brushed past her and rushed out onto the porch. Hermann had caught Bessie; the girl was hysterical. Her knees were bleeding and her clothes covered with dust. Helen dashed toward them; her breathing had become a series of brief gasps. She fell on her knees and grabbed Bessie by the shoulders.

"Tell us exactly what happened."

Bessie opened her mouth, and the words spilled out in quick succession. Helen had to remind her several times to slow down.

"We were up in the woods where the blackberry bushes are. There weren't any blackberries left except a few dried-up ones. I put one in my mouth and..."

"Yes, yes, but what about Anne?" Helen interrupted impatiently.

"Anne saw a rabbit and chased after it. After a while, I realized that she had been gone a long time, and I called her. I searched the area when I found her basket on the ground."

"Where's the basket?" Helen's voice trembled, and her pulse throbbed erratically.

"Uh, I don't know. I must have left it there. I got so scared and ran away."

The colonel had been in hushed conversation with Anneliese, who translated Bessie's words. He turned on his heels, raced up the steps, and disappeared into the cottage. They heard him speak into his radio. He emerged with his car keys in hand, said something to Anneliese, and ran toward the gate.

"Here, Dad, you take care of Bessie. I'm going with him," Helen said and ran after the colonel.

Anneliese turned to Hermann and said, "The colonel has called for help. Don't worry; he will find your granddaughter. I'm going to attend to Bessie's bloody knees." She took Bessie's hand and led her up the steps.

Hermann hesitated for a moment and then, with the help of his cane, hobbled through the gate as fast as his limp would allow, made a left-hand turn and proceeded down the hill.

The colonel scaled the uphill path with rapid strides. When Helen caught up with him, he shot her an approving glance.

When he jumped into the jeep, Helen said, "Let's search the forest first. I know where the blackberry patch is located."

He stared at her quizzically but suggested she led the way. When they reached the blackberry patch, they found Bessie's basket on the ground. They kept searching the area until they discovered the second basket. The colonel kneeled and checked the ground. He raised two fingers. Helen understood there were two sets of footprints: one child and one adult. The colonel explained to her that the tracks were hard to read. They followed them as far as possible; the colonel finally turned and shrugged his shoulders. "Let's go back to the jeep."

As soon as they entered the clearing, they saw Hermann clamoring up the hill. He was waving frantically. The colonel jumped into the jeep. Helen watched anxiously as it thundered down the path, spitting gravel and whipping up dirt that gathered into a honey-colored dust cloud. When the colonel reached Hermann, he got out of the jeep, picked him up with ease, and deposited him gently on the passenger seat. Hermann's face was bright red and bathed in perspiration.

"The Gypsies are gone!" he cried. The colonel looked at him, not comprehending.

"The cave is empty. The Gypsies are gone. They took Anne. I know it."

The colonel put his hand on Hermann's arm and gave it a gentle squeeze. "We will find her." He shifted into reverse; the tires spun, and the jeep barreled up the hill and came to a screeching halt in front of the gate where Helen was waiting. Hermann scrambled out of the jeep as Anneliese came running from the cottage and handed the colonel the two-way radio.

"The Gypsies are gone..." Hermann's voice broke.

"Dad, what are you saying?" Helen stiffened in anticipation of his next words.

"I'm saying that they took her. It's no coincidence that Anne and the Gypsies disappeared at the same time. They were at the cave when we passed there earlier today."

"Oh my God..." Helen swayed, and Anneliese quickly extended a steadying arm. Helen covered her mouth to keep from screaming. The Gypsies had a reputation for snatching up children, who were never seen again. She wanted to die; she just could not bear the pain.

"Helen, listen to me," the colonel said firmly. "We are going to find Anne, I promise you that."

He had spoken in English and she understood based on his tone, and just shook her head. Tears streamed down her face. Bessie tugged at her arm.

"Mutti, I believe the colonel. He'll find her. I know it, and you must believe it too."

Helen looked into the pleading eyes of her older daughter and pulled her into her arms. She sobbed quietly as she buried her face in Bessie's hair. When she looked up, her eyes met Hermann's. They were filled with compassion and love. He reached out, and they came together in a small circle. Like so many times before, they joined hands. The colonel stood and watched. Anneliese pulled him into the circle, and they bowed their heads and prayed.

The rumbling of an army truck announced its arrival at the parking pad. The colonel pulled away from them and ran up the hill. Eight soldiers emerged from the vehicle. They had brought two German shepherd dogs, who were straining at their leashes. They gathered around the colonel. One of the soldiers left the group and jogged down the hill to speak with Anneliese.

"He needs something that belongs to Anne. The dogs need to catch her scent," she interpreted.

Helen ran toward the bicycles, retrieved a sweater from the backseat, and handed it to the soldier. He tipped his helmet and took off to join the others. The colonel barked his orders, and the men disappeared into the forest with the yelping dogs leading the way.

"There isn't much time." Hermann pointed toward the horizon. The sun hovered at the point of beginning its slow descent. "They can't keep up the search in the dark."

"Remember, they have the dogs. Let's go into the house, and I'll make some fresh coffee," Anneliese suggested.

"Rosa will be worried if we don't show up soon. I'm going into town. I must tell her what has happened. We'll return tomorrow morning." Hermann hugged them all. "God help us," he said and swung his body over the bike. When he reached the gate, he got down and pushed the bike up the hill. Then he turned left and disappeared.

Helen fought a growing sense of panic as she paced the front porch. The sun had disappeared long ago. She shivered. Dusk had brought a chilly dampness. Anne did not have her sweater and would be so cold. How were they going to find her in the dark? The Gypsies were familiar with these woods and knew where to hide, leaving the soldiers at a disadvantage. What if the Gypsies hurt Anne? Helen's heart pounded, and she could feel her stomach churn. If they lost Anne, Fritz would never get to know his daughter. Her mind was filled with a fear that consumed all sense of reason, and then she remembered the dogs. *The dogs will find Anne, but what if they don't?* Her hands flew to her face to muffle her anguished sobs.

Anneliese appeared in the doorway. She turned on the newly installed porch light. It radiated a golden, protective glow.

"It's past midnight. Why don't you lie down a while?" she said.

Helen wiped her face. "I can't sleep, not a wink, but I will take a cup of tea."

"Okay." Anneliese disappeared into the kitchen. When she returned, she was carrying two cups. She handed one of them to Helen. "I just checked on Bessie; she's sleeping soundly."

Helen stared down into the valley, where Wildenheim lay peacefully. Isolated lights glittered in the night.

"My fiancé died at Warsaw. We were to be married on his next leave." Anneliese stood next to her. The words came haltingly. "My father and brother are reported missing. My mother has never been the same. She keeps talking about the past." She smiled at Helen. "You have a wonderful family. I wanted to have children with Heinz…"

Helen burst into tears. Anneliese put her arms around her.

The colonel pointed the flashlight at his watch, ten past midnight. The moon had slipped behind thick clouds, which complicated their rescue mission. The silence was incredible, broken only by the occasional sound of an animal aroused from sleep. He had divided his men into two groups, and they kept in touch via radio. So far, there was no sign of Anne or the Gypsies. The dog strained at the leash, his nose to the ground, but he had not picked up a scent. The colonel's thoughts went to the family back at the cottage. They had endured the darkest times and had remained steadfast in their courage and fortitude, but he recognized their vulnerability. He had to face the fact that they might not find Anne. The Gypsies were elusive, like shadows in the night that melted into the trees. He was suddenly overcome with an incredible desire to see his daughters, to wrap his arms around them and tell them how much he loved them. He clenched his fists and picked up his pace.

The soldiers arrived at an open field. The dog pushed on past a rock quarry filled with clear water. The narrow trail led them back into the forest and curled in an uphill climb. The soldiers breathed hard as they tried to keep up with the dog. It would stop periodically and raise its head; eyes fixed straight ahead in an immovable stare, and then press on with a brief yap. As they approached the summit, the moon appeared briefly. The colonel signaled his men to stop. He scanned the area. The outline of a fortress rose through the trees. The dog became agitated; he yelped and strained at his leash. The men trudged ahead until they reached a courtyard surrounded by deteriorating walls, the only remains of the stronghold erected almost a thousand years ago. The dog acted strangely and seemed confused. He had his nose close to the ground, gave a brief bark and sat on his hind legs, and refused to budge. The colonel bellowed a command, and the men spread out to check the area.

The first appearance of daylight announced the new morning. Anneliese put the kettle on the stove and then turned out the lights in the kitchen and living room. She tiptoed past Helen, who sat at the table, her head slumped on her arms. Anneliese entered the back bedroom to check on Bessie. She peered through the doorway just as Bessie turned in bed and gave her a brief smile, which was quickly replaced by an immense sadness that swept across her face. She swung her legs out of bed.

"Any news of Anne?"

"No, sweetheart." Anneliese handed Bessie her shoes. "We'll hear something soon. How about a cup of cocoa?"

Bessie's eyes lit up. "Cocoa? Oh yes, I'd love some." She finished tying her shoelaces and followed Anneliese into the kitchen. When they walked past Helen, she raised her head.

"What time is it?"

Just then, the kitchen clock struck the seventh hour. Helen stared out the window. The sun's rays caressed her face. Across the walkway, a rabbit nibbled on Rosa's marigolds in the flower garden.

"I'm going to fix some pancakes," Anneliese said to Bessie.

"And cocoa," Bessie added, and Anneliese smiled.

Helen kept watching the rabbit. His ears shot up, and he sat still for a second and then dashed into the bushes. Helen cried out sharply and bolted out the door, followed by Anneliese and Bessie. Helen ran down the path just as the colonel walked through the gate. In his arms, he cradled the limp body of a strange child in familiar clothing. Helen almost collided with the colonel. He handed her the bundle. Anne reached for her mother, who hugged her so tightly, she cried out.

"Oh, I'm so sorry, sweetheart, but..." Helen paused and looked at Anne. Her face and arms had been darkened with what appeared to be shoe polish. Her blue eyes contrasted sharply with her blackened face. Her short red hair was saturated with a black, greasy substance that transformed her curls into rigid spikes. Helen suppressed a smile when she realized that Anne was unharmed and carried her back to the cottage.

"Anne, you look like a grease monkey," Bessie said and burst out laughing but quickly ran for cover when Anne wriggled out of her mother's arms and chased after her vowing vengeance. Helen's laughter rang through the quiet morning, releasing all tension and flooding her with relief as she watched her daughters chase each other. She turned to the colonel.

"She seems to be just fine. How do I ever thank you?" She reached out with both hands, and the colonel pulled her to him and held her close.

"Your prayers helped," he said simply.

They were gathered around the living room table. They had had their fill of pancakes and coffee. Anne had had a good wash and looked more like herself again. She had experienced a great scare, but now that it was all behind her, and she had been safely reunited with her family, she was excited to talk about her adventure. The Gypsies had frightened her initially, but treated her kindly, and she wanted to keep the gaudy necklace they had draped around her neck.

The colonel lit a cigarette and, aided by Anneliese's translation, told the story. They had combed the woods for hours when they reached the top of the mountain. There, they found the ruins of an ancient fortress.

"Wasselburg," Helen said.

"I had never seen it before," the colonel said. "The location is a strategic masterpiece. Only outside walls remain standing, but the chapel still has a partial roof and steps leading inside. We found

Anne sleeping on the stone floor by a dying fire. We searched the area, but there was no sign of the Gypsies."

"They must have heard the dog and rushed off. They knew their fate if they got caught," Anneliese said.

Helen strolled through the orchard. There was an isolated apple they had missed during the harvest. She reached up, plucked it, and took a hearty bite.

"These apples have an unusual taste." The colonel had joined her. "Kind of tart and crisp, like our Granny Smith apples."

"Granny Smith?"

"My wife used to make apple pies with Granny Smith apples. Actually, I believe she mixed different apples…" The words drifted with the wind, and he became silent as they continued walking beneath the trees. "I miss my daughters. They're growing up without me," he finally said, "and I miss their mother, more than I'd ever imagined," he added with a hint of sarcasm in his voice.

"It seems that we have much in common, Colonel Blake. I miss Fritz so much. The children haven't seen him for several years. I fear that they will not remember him."

"You will never allow that to happen." He smiled broadly at her. "You are a strong woman, and I admire your courage. Your husband is a lucky man."

"It's all a farce," Helen said. "I put on a front. For the children." She paused and then added, "I keep focused on the day when Fritz will return. He's got to come back to us."

"Of course." The colonel squeezed her hand reassuringly.

"Do you believe in unconditional forgiveness?" he asked after a while.

He surprised her with the question. She deliberated her answer for a moment and said, "Yes, I do." She glanced at him sideways. He remained silent and stared grimly ahead.

The crunching gravel alerted them. Rosa pushed the bike through the gate, and Hermann limped beside her leaning heavily on his cane. Helen chuckled inwardly at the thought of Rosa peddling the bike with Hermann on the rear seat.

"Have you found her?" Rosa called out, breathless.

At that moment, Anne dashed down the porch steps and ran into her grandmother's arms. "Thank God you're safe." Rosa gave her a bear hug. "Are you all right, sweetheart?" She examined Anne's face. The hairline above her forehead showed faint traces of black. "What's that?" Before Anne could answer, Rosa announced, "My dear child, you need a bath," and she took Anne's hand and led her into the house. Hermann stood still as he watched and smiled.

"Breakfast is ready," Anneliese called out the kitchen window.

Helen answered the doorbell. The colonel bowed and kissed her hand. She invited him into the living room where Hermann and Rosa were relaxing with a weak cup of coffee. They had resumed the German tradition of mid-afternoon coffee or tea. Thanks to the extra income, they had stopped using the same coffee grounds repeatedly. The colonel declined Helen's offer for a cup and sat down. Helen joined her mother on the sofa, and they looked at him expectantly.

"I have some news…" He began hesitantly. His German was much improved. He fidgeted with his hat and continued, "I've received my orders. I'm going home next week."

"That's wonderful!" Rosa exclaimed. "You must be thrilled."

The sadness in the colonel's facial expression seemed to indicate otherwise. *He doesn't want to leave Anneliese*, Helen thought. *Poor Anneliese.* Helen wondered if he had already told her.

"I'm going to Hermann's Ruhe directly from here to remove my belongings. I will hide the key behind the shutters at the rear bedroom window." He paused and swallowed hard. "I want to thank you again for allowing me to live at your cottage. It was the best time I spent in Europe." He rose abruptly.

"Please...just a minute." Hermann pleaded as he shuffled over to the desk and opened a drawer. He pulled out an envelope and handed it to the colonel.

"What's this?"

"We want to return some of the rent money. We're so grateful for what you've done at Hermann's Ruhe, running the electricity, leveling the parking pad, but most of all giving us Anne back. We'll be forever in your debt." He pushed the envelope into the colonel's hands.

"I don't want this..." The colonel tried to give the envelope back to Hermann, who threw up his arms in protest.

"I am afraid we must insist," Hermann said, and Helen and Rosa nodded in agreement. Hermann reached out and clasped the colonel's hand in both of his. "Good-bye and God bless," he said. The colonel bowed his head and turned to Rosa who gave him a loving hug.

"Thank you for everything. We'll miss you," she said.

When he turned to Helen, he hesitated, but she reached out and embraced him warmly. "Thank you for giving me my daughter back," she whispered. The colonel clung to her. When he pulled away, he cleared his throat. He bowed and smiled through misty eyes. Hermann accompanied him to the door.

One last wave and he skipped down the steps and climbed into the jeep. He started the engine and then reached inside his coat pocket and pulled out the tattered letter. The ink was smudged. He had read it many times. Katie had answered his long letter by return mail. She said to hurry home; she and the girls were waiting for him.

Fall was coming to an end. There had been a touch of frost during the night, which lingered in glistening silvery bands on the tree branches, a subtle hint of winter waiting in the wings. Helen inhaled the crisp air deeply. She pushed her bike through the gate, followed by Hermann and Rosa. At the end of the path, the little cottage beckoned. Helen turned to Hermann, he smiled and his pace picked up. *This place always lifts us up,* Helen thought. *It's as close to heaven as it gets.*

They unlocked the front door and gasped. The kitchen had been outfitted with a small refrigerator. There was a basket filled with fruit and packaged goods sitting on the counter. Hermann stepped into the living room. His eyes fell on a vase filled with fresh-cut flowers sitting on the table, and then he spotted the envelope and tore it open. Sheets of paper currency spilled to the floor.

"Helen, Rosa, look at this," he said and pulled out the note. The two women rushed from the kitchen where they had been examining the treasures in the basket. They looked over Hermann's shoulder, and he began to read.

Dear Friends,

Thank you with all my heart for allowing me to stay at your beautiful cottage. You will never know how much spending time at Hermann's Ruhe has meant to me. For the first time in years, there is peace in my heart. I am sorry to have to leave, but I will return to my country with fond memories, as my family awaits me.

It has been a privilege to get to know all of you. You have taught me much, and I salute your valor.

It was signed by the colonel.

They stared at each other in silence. Hermann blinked. "What an extraordinary person. Having met him gives me hope that mankind can forget its differences and someday live together in peace."

A rabbit hopped across the porch. It paused and peered through the open door. The three people inside seemed preoccupied, and it dashed down the steps toward Rosa's flower garden where the forbidden marigolds beckoned in glorious splendor.

7

The Homecoming

Spring had arrived, and the warmer temperatures were a welcome relief from the blustery cold that had prevailed for most of the winter. They had stretched their rationed fuel supply during the long, bitter months and kept only the fire in the kitchen stove going. They went to bed early and huddled beneath the down comforters in the chilly bedrooms.

The roses in the flower garden had weathered the snow and ice and were now bursting with blossoms. A gentle breeze carried the delicate fragrance through the open kitchen window.

Helen raised her head and sniffed the air. She had slaved over the washboard all morning and decided to take a break. She sat down and looked at her red, cracked hands with disgust. Fritz had always admired her long, tapered fingers and the velvety softness of her hands. *If he ever comes home, he won't recognize me. He'll wonder who this old woman is,* she thought with a grim smile.

"I'm going into the forest." Rosa came into the kitchen and reached for the wicker basket. Helen remained silent and gazed out the window. A robin was busy building her nest in the peach tree in the backyard. There would be little ones soon. A new cycle had begun, but not for her; she was stuck in limbo. She couldn't imagine a future without Fritz, and yet she might have to. Her fate had long been decided, and she would be the last to know.

"What's the matter? You've said very little all morning." Rosa stepped closer and examined her daughter's face with a critical eye.

Helen took off her glasses and rubbed her eyes. "I'm worried about Fritz…the children…our future. I may have to face the fact that Fritz will never come home." A whimpering sound rose in her throat, and her mouth began to tremble. "Not knowing is driving me mad."

Rosa's eyes flashed with fire. "Now listen up, girl. You've hung on this far and can't lose the faith now. Unless you're told otherwise, you must assume that Fritz is still alive," she said firmly.

"It gets more difficult each day. No matter how hard I fight it, I'm losing hope. I get so depressed. Most days, I have to force myself to get out of bed in the morning." Her hand brushed across her nose. "Mr. Brenner told me about the bloody battles at Huertgen Forest near the Belgian border. What if Fritz had been fighting there?"

"I would like to know where Mr. Brenner gets this information when no one else knows what's happening." Rosa made no attempt to hide her exasperation.

"He said the casualties numbered in the tens of thousands," Helen whispered.

"Look, we don't know where Fritz is, and it's a mistake to speculate. The Brenners take perverted pleasure in upsetting you. Don't listen to them." Rosa patted her daughter on the shoulder and left.

Helen leaned back in her chair, pulled out a handkerchief, and dabbed at her eyes. Voices reached her from the hallway, and she raised her head. Her heart began to pound, and she jumped up and ran out of the kitchen. She pulled the apartment door open and stood opposite Edwin Stringer, Mary's husband. His threadbare uniform fell from his shoulders like a cloak, and a sturdy rope encircled his waist and kept his pants in place. An angry red scar trailed from his forehead down his temple and settled into his left cheek. His thick black hair had turned gray. Helen stared at him in momentary confusion and then peered over his shoulder. She saw an Allied jeep outside, backing out of the driveway.

"Oh, Edwin..." She mouthed the words. His gaunt face approached her, and she fainted.

"Helen, can you hear me?"

Helen opened her eyes and looked into Mary's worried face. Her head was spinning as she rested against Edwin who had caught her just in time. His thin arms were around her.

"I'm all right." Helen straightened up. She looked at Edwin. "For a minute..."

"I know; you thought I was Fritz." He released her and said, "I'm sorry, but I've no news about Fritz, but maybe he too is on his way home. They told us at the last minute that we were being released. It looks like the Americans are freeing all prisoners of war."

"Edwin, I'm so happy that you've come home. Mary and I have prayed for this day." Helen's eyes swept over his scrawny body. "You're going to need some fattening up," she added with a faint smile.

"I'm going to have to take it slow. My stomach has shrunk to the size of a thimble..." he said, looking vacantly into space. The two women watched him anxiously. Then he blinked and said, "By the way, Werner and I came home together. We were able to hitch a ride from a GI. We were shocked to see Werner's house has been leveled. He's checking the site right now. I guess Inge and the children are with his parents."

"Edwin, no...they aren't..." Mary's voice broke. She swallowed hard and said, "Their house received a direct hit during a night air strike. They were all killed, except for Ben, Inge's dog..."

"I've got to go to Werner." Edwin pushed her aside and rushed out the door. The women followed.

Two houses down, Werner sat on the rubble that used to be his home, his face covered with his remaining left hand. The empty right sleeve of his tattered uniform fluttered in the breeze. Several neighbors had gathered.

"Werner, I'm so sorry." Edwin reached out to the tormented man.

"My family is gone." Werner raised his fist up to the sky. "God...why take them and not me?" He dropped his arm and sobbed. He shook his head. "Someone...please tell me...why? I should have died many times in battle..." His voice drowned in his tears and he wept aloud rocking back and forth.

Helen sat next to him and pulled him close. His head dropped onto her shoulder as his body convulsed with grief. Some people turned and left, crying openly. They could not comfort him; they were still trying to deal with their own pain.

"Werner, your parents and your sister are safe. We'll take you to them," Helen said, and when Werner did not respond, Edwin reached out and pulled him up by his remaining arm.

"Come," Edwin said and led him away.

A tantalizing aroma filled the kitchen. Helen had just finished decorating the cake. Shaped like a porcupine with alternating layers of cake and chocolate frosting, it was covered with slivered almonds. She examined her creation with a critical eye. Birthdays were a big deal for the family, and there was always a porcupine cake. This time, it was Anne's turn. She would turn six tomorrow. Trina and Mia, her two dolls, had disappeared a week ago and were now hidden in Helen's closet, wearing brand-new clothes she and Rosa had sewn from fabric scraps. Hermann was able to swap a pair of binoculars on the black market for an old wooden scooter and had spent the past week sanding and painting. The wheels were badly worn and needed replacing, so Mr. Stringer donated the wheels of his broken-down wooden cart. They were a bit large but in fair condition. The scooter, freshly painted in apple green, the only paint Hermann could lay his hands on, was safely stored out of sight at the Stringers' apartment. Anne had been asking for a scooter for so long, and Helen was thrilled that they were able to grant her wish.

She glanced out the kitchen window. Edwin and Mary were working in their vegetable garden. Mary was on her knees planting seedlings, when Edwin pulled her up into an embrace and kissed her. Twinges of jealousy tugged at Helen's heart. She fought hard to dismiss them. She didn't begrudge them their happiness. Her fate was sealed, and she must accept it and be content with the wonderful memories she and Fritz had shared. He had given her three beautiful children who would be his legacy, and she would raise them to make him proud.

Anne kneeled on the sidewalk. The sunshine reflected in the glossy green paint of her scooter, which was resting on the ground next to her. She was waiting for her friend Lilli to come out and play. She was softly humming her favorite song and drawing pictures in the sand, when she spotted a man in the distance. He walked slowly, and when he came closer, she noticed he wore a ragged uniform which seemed way too big. He carried his left arm in a sling, and his head was swathed in white bandages. A few stubborn strands of black hair had escaped the dressing and stuck straight up in the air. He stopped in front of her and searched her face with gaunt eyes. Anne cringed as she stared at his full black beard. She jumped to her feet, backed up and fled toward the house, just as the front door opened, and her mother appeared.

Helen stood transfixed. She brought both hands to her cheeks and cried, "Oh my God..." She kept repeating the words as she ran down the steps toward the man and threw herself into his arms.

Anne watched with big eyes as the two people alternately laughed, cried, hugged, and kissed. Her mother was behaving strangely. She crept closer and tugged at Helen's apron. Helen turned around and lifted her up. Her tear-streaked face glowed, and she whispered, "Anne, this is your father."

The man smiled through a blinding mist that swam across his eyes. He reached out to touch her red curls. She pulled away. She kicked and screamed until her mother put her down. "You're supposed to be dead! I heard them talk about you. You're dead!" She scampered up the steps and disappeared into the house.

Fritz swayed, but Helen held him steady. "She doesn't remember you. You're a stranger to her. She needs time to adjust."

Fritz kept shaking his head. "That's not the welcome I had expected," he said bitterly. "The only thing that kept me going day after day was the thought of my family waiting for my return. Each time I closed my eyes, I saw your faces. You were close enough to touch. That's how I survived."

"Oh, Fritz, don't worry about Anne. This was a shock to her. She was a baby the last time you saw her. All she knows is the pictures I have shown her, and frankly, you look very different with that beard. Give her a little time, and she'll come around. I'm so grateful to have you back. I've had no word from you for so long." She hugged him to her.

"I've been laid up in an American field hospital. When a bullet scraped my temple and shrapnel shattered my arm, I thought that was it. I was certain I would bleed to death on the battlefield, but when I woke up, I found myself lying on a cot, and a nurse told me that American soldiers had brought me in. I had several operations. The American surgeon saved my life.

I spent many months in the care of the Americans. I was their prisoner, but they treated me kindly; however, no correspondence was allowed."

Helen shuddered and sent off a quick prayer. Bless the Americans. She was never going to think ill of them again, even though they were occupying her town. "It's been tough around here too, believe me," she said as she led him up the steps.

The long nights in the shelter and the constant battle to fight starvation now seemed insignificant compared to the intense days and weeks that followed Fritz's return. Paul and Bessie adjusted quickly, but Anne refused to have anything to do with her father. She screamed when he touched her. At dinnertime, she insisted on sitting at the far end of the table. When she snuck across the hall at night, she found the bedroom door closed. She crept back to her bed with a hateful heart, crying herself to sleep. On those occasions when she was allowed in the big bed, she curled up close to her mother, keeping as far away from Fritz as possible.

"Anne is too old to be sleeping in our bed," Fritz complained.

"I know, but she has nightmares that frighten her terribly. Please be patient," Helen pleaded.

"Everyone has nightmares."

"Anne is only six years old and too young to understand the horrors of war, but she has experienced the fear. You don't have a clue what's been going on around here while you were away." Helen struggled to keep her voice calm.

"Honey, I'm sorry." He rushed toward her and pulled her into his arms. "I guess none of us will ever be the same."

"We must be patient. It'll take time. We're alive, and that's all that matters." She brushed her face against his and kissed him.

"Mutti, Opa...come quick!" Paul's voice was frantic. Helen hurried into the kitchen, followed by Hermann. Fritz was on the floor, curled into a fetal position with his eyes turned back. Helen raced into their bedroom and grabbed the serum and syringe.

"Paul, push up his shirtsleeve..." she cried as she knelt down. She stuck the needle into his upper arm. She held her breath for the next several agonizing seconds; soon, his eyelids began to flutter, and he looked at them in confusion. He complained of being dizzy when they helped him sit up.

"Darling, how do you feel?" Helen asked softly.

"I think I'm okay." He looked exhausted but refused their support as he slowly got to his feet. "I can manage," he said as he leaned against the table. "They told me that I could have seizures that come without warning. I had a couple at the field hospital but thought that was it." He straightened up. "I'm awfully tired. I think I'll lie down for a while." He left the kitchen.

"Stay with him, Helen," Hermann urged, "just in case he has another one."

"Dad, I'm worried. Fritz tosses and turns in his sleep. He often cries out and then wakes up, with his body bathed in sweat."

"Helen, the nightmares will haunt him for a long time, believe me. After all these years, I still get them. You must be patient," Hermann said. "Didn't the doctor tell him that seizures would be rare and eventually disappear altogether?"

"But it's been six months..." She paused and released a sharp breath.

"Hopefully, this was the last one. Now go." Hermann gently pushed her out the kitchen door.

Helen and Rosa were on their knees weeding the flower beds. Helen had been unusually quiet. Rosa watched her from the corner of her eye. She knew that there was something weighing heavily on her daughter's mind.

"I asked Fritz what happened at Huertgen Forest." Helen finally spoke. "He said there were huge casualties. Men were blown to bits. He would stumble across a foot, an arm, or a body so mangled it was unidentifiable. At first, he would gag, but soon he just trudged forward with the rest of the men. He said he didn't believe that he would survive the slaughter. He also said that this battle served no purpose whatsoever other than killing soldiers on both sides."

"War is a waste of lives, the destruction of nations," Rosa said. "It has been so since time began; one country conquers another."

"Fritz sees the Americans as liberators, not conquerors."

"How did the Americans treat him?" Rosa asked.

"He has no complaints. The doctors set his arm. His head wound required two operations. I could tell that he didn't want to talk about it, and he begged me not to press him further," Helen said.

"Your father was the same way," Rosa said with a sigh. "Each time I questioned him about the war; he changed the subject or left the room on some pretense, and finally, I gave up asking questions." Rosa sat back on her heels. "We can't possibly imagine the horror our men have experienced. I guess talking about it brings it all back. War has changed all of us, but the most devastating effect has been on our men who survived and came back and now must make the difficult transition into a normal life. They deserve all our compassion and support."

The relationship between Anne and her father had not improved. Anne's rejection of him was laced with jealousy, which became apparent to those around her. She would watch little exchanges of affection between her parents with a grim face. No matter how much Rosa and Hermann tried to plead with her, Anne insisted that she hated her father. On the surface, Fritz took it all in stride and kept his feelings to himself. He must wait until she came to him. It was the only way they could have a relationship.

On occasion, Anne would spy on her father. Such was the case early one afternoon. She hid behind the peach tree in the backyard and observed him building a fence around the bomb crater. She had heard him say to her mother that the water level rose each time it rained and could pose a threat for Anne and Lilli, who did not know how to swim.

Anne squatted on her heels and studied his face. The bandage around his head had long been removed along with the ugly beard. He looked more like the man in the picture on her mother's dresser—the man she had vowed to hate. Her mother seemed so happy these days and never cried anymore. Anne had noticed that he was being exceptionally nice to her. He had made her a slingshot, and she had allowed him to show her how to use it. It was a much finer sling shot than Lilli's.

When he played chess with her grandfather, and she walked into the room, he always invited her to take his place. Just the other day, he challenged her to a game. She eyed him suspiciously but agreed. She beat him fair and square, and he beamed at her.

"Great game, Anne, I'm proud of you," he had said.

"Anne is a worthy opponent and knows how to plan her strategies," Hermann said. "You should see her roller-skate."

Fritz hesitated for moment and then asked softly, "May I join you the next time you skate?"

She considered his question and agreed.

"I guess so, although I haven't skated in a long time. Paul and Bessie used to skate with me, but they got bored." After a moment's pause, she added, "It's no fun...skating alone."

During the following weeks, he often joined her, and she discovered that he was an excellent skater, even better than Paul. He taught her how to come to a perfect stop without crashing into the wall. He knew how to skate backward and do the spread eagle, but when he reached out to help her loosen her skate, she turned away, and she saw his hand drop to his side.

Anne resented it when Bessie sat next to him on the sofa, deeply immersed in discussion about cooking, Bessie's favorite topic. Bessie always gave her father a big hug before she went to bed at night. Anne looked upon Bessie with contempt; she was a traitor. Paul, on the other hand, seemed to struggle with some problems of his own regarding his father. Anne recalled a conversation she had witnessed between Paul and Mutti in the vegetable garden shortly after Fritz's return.

"Papa treats me like a child. I know he doesn't mean to, but..."

"Oh, Paul, your father knows what a tremendous support you have been to all of us and that I never could have managed without you. Don't forget that you were only twelve the last time he was home on leave. Circumstances have forced you to grow up much too soon. He loves you and is terribly proud of you," Helen said.

"All of the men in this family must work together. We're a team." Hermann appeared from behind the apple tree where he had been working on the supports for the tomato plants. "There is much to be done and much to be thankful for," he said.

"I know," Paul agreed.

Anne rose to her feet. She deliberated her options and decided to sneak away before her father discovered her. She took one last look; he had disappeared. She hurried closer and saw he had collapsed in the dirt. He didn't move. She had heard her mother discussing his seizures with her grandfather. She knew that if he didn't get his medication quickly, he might die. She turned and ran toward the house screaming, "Mutti! Mutti!" She hammered the door with both fists. Helen tore the door open.

"Papa...needs medicine..." Anne sobbed. Helen raced to the bedroom, snatched the vial and syringe from the night table, and followed Anne. When they reached Fritz, Helen's hands shook as she filled the syringe. Anne unbuttoned his shirtsleeve and pushed it up. Helen jabbed the needle into the skin. His face was pale, and his breath passed noiselessly through his nostrils. The muddy water in the crater reached up to his knees, and they gently moved his legs to a dry place. They peered anxiously into his face. Helen stroked his rumpled hair and took his limp hand in hers.

"Hang on, darling. Don't leave me now. I can't bear to lose you again. I need you desperately; your family needs you." She brought his hand to her cheek.

"Papa, can you hear me? It's Anne," Anne pleaded with tears in her eyes. "I know I've behaved dreadfully. I'm sorry. I love you so much..." She cried openly. Helen pulled her close, and Anne raised her tear-streaked face. "Did Papa hear me?"

"Yes, sweetheart," Helen said confidently. "He heard every word."

Fritz stirred and opened his eyes. His wife and daughter were looking at him with distraught faces that changed quickly into smiles of relief and joy.

"What happened?" he asked slowly.

"Anne just saved your life," Helen said.

Fritz turned to his daughter, and she came into his arms and snuggled against his chest. He looked across the fuzzy red head at his wife and smiled. Helen wrapped her arms around both of them. She knew that the circle was finally complete. They were a real family again.

8

A Time of Peace

August 7, 1957

The little boy in the framed photo had a dimpled smile. The sandy thatch of hair would surely darken in time, just like Paul's had done, and the incredible hazel eyes that changed color at a whim, so much like Fritz's, were his legacy from the two men most dear to her heart. Helen pondered the picture as she lingered at her dressing table. Then she looked up and studied her reflection in the mirror. She grimaced, exposing her teeth. She was fortunate to have been able to hold on to all of them despite the many years lacking a proper diet and dental care. She relaxed her mouth and tucked her chin in. The years had been good to her. There were plenty of wrinkles, but she didn't care. Her hair, now totally gray, had retained its fullness and curl while her body had lost all its sharp edges and filled in at the right places. She chuckled as she stared at her image from behind bifocal spectacles, another sign of the passing of time.

"Are you getting ready?" Fritz stood behind her. Dressed in a three-piece suit, he wore the sea-foam silk tie she had given him for his birthday last month. His thinning hair had been carefully combed, and he smelled of Old Spice aftershave. He leaned over and brushed his face against hers.

"Isn't he precious?" She said, lifting her eyes. "Our first grandchild. The resemblance to you and Paul is stunning."

"So you keep saying." Fritz stepped back and evaluated Helen's face in the mirror. "Frankly, I'm not sure, but I do know that he's got your prominent Greek nose." He kissed the top of her head. "Now, finish dressing or we'll be late for our grandson's first birthday party."

"I'll be ready in a minute," Helen said, and he turned and left the room. She counted her blessings often these days. It was a miracle that Fritz survived the war, but when he came back, she noticed he had changed. He hid his scars well and was adamant in refusing to talk about his ordeal. She never pressed him; she had to deal with her own painful memories of that terrible time. Her emotions were often guided by the past, and she struggled to move beyond the nightmare that had been her life for so long and had forced her to operate daily as an automaton, focusing only on the survival of her family. She was ashamed of some of the things she had done and could never tell Fritz. She guessed that he sensed her inner struggles but did not question her. He had insisted that they make a pact to start living their lives free of the constraints of the past.

Helen's constant concern over the impact the war might have had on the young, impressive minds of her children proved to be baseless, as they were thriving without any debilitating effects from the past. Even Rosa had moved on and never looked back.

Helen was reaching for her hairbrush when her eyes fell on the picture of her parents, a snapshot that had been taken in the summer of 1939 and which she had later enlarged. Hermann and Rosa stood hand in hand beneath the carved plaque at Hermann's Ruhe. Her eyes welled. "Oh, Dad," she whispered. "I miss you so much. We survived the blazes of hell, only to have you taken away two short years later."

It was in early 1947 when Hermann was first diagnosed with colon cancer. After surgery that necessitated a colostomy, he found his quality of life severely limited. He became impatient and irritable. Even Anne was unable to interest him in a game of chess. He fell into a depression and withdrew from everyone. When he gently slipped away in his sleep only six months later, Rosa said that he was finally at peace. Helen was devastated, and Rosa became the beacon that led the family through the difficult days before and after the funeral. She dealt with her grief by keeping busy and, at age seventy-five, resumed her volunteer work at the hospital where she inspired the young nurses by setting an example of working tirelessly while keeping an even disposition and remaining true to the no-nonsense attitude that had dominated her entire life.

Helen rose and walked over to the closet. Wearing a full slip and nylon stockings, her hands brushed over the garments neatly placed on hangers; the shelf below held a variety of shoes. She would never forget the time when she wore nothing but rags and was happy to have them. Gone were the days when she took apart her dresses and made them into clothing for the children. Life was good, but she could never forget the hardships. Over Fritz's protests, she still operated every day in a frugality mode that declared many of the luxuries now available to them as being wasteful.

After Fritz had returned from the war, they began reconstructing their business. The process was slow, and their days were filled with hard work that often extended late into the night. Everyone in the family pitched in. Franz, Fritz's father, organized the piecemeal reconstruction of the office and the warehouse, which had received extensive damage during the air attacks, while Helen and Bessie learned all about furniture refinishing as they refurbished the desks and filing cabinets that Fritz had assembled from scrap wood.

Hermann and Fritz would commute via bicycle in all kinds of weather to call on the clothing manufacturers in the region to resume business relationships. The Schmidt reputation always preceded them, and, in due course, the company grew and became once more the thriving enterprise it had been before the war.

In the summer of 1950, the foundation for their house was laid, and they moved in a year later. Although small, the house offered more space than the apartment they had shared with her parents on Ludwigstrasse.

After Paul had graduated from the university in 1953, he joined the firm, and he and Fritz continued to expand the supply lines to meet the growing textile demands of the clothing factories in the area. The creativity and drive Paul exhibited as a teenager were even more pronounced in the adult. He was a total optimist, and, unlike Helen, he retained no bitterness or regrets at the cards that were dealt him, which had deprived him of a good part of his youth.

Gossip blossomed in Wildenheim, and eyebrows were raised when he fell in love with a Polish refugee, a lovely girl whose even-tempered personality blended beautifully into their family of volatile temperaments. The Nazis had killed her parents, and she and her brother had fled Poland with nothing but the clothes on their backs. On a balmy day in June, Fritz proudly walked her down the isle of the newly restored Sacred Heart Church, which was filled with their friends and curious spectators.

The reception took place at their beloved Hermann's Ruhe, where Bessie and Rosa created a buffet table spread with delectables, such as venison salad with apples and cucumbers, pate made with finely chopped liver, roasted chicken, bruschetta, and Fritz's favorite, rollmops, a combination of salted herring and thinly sliced onions. The dessert table was Anne's favorite. The tantalizing array of apple strudel, Black Forest torte, cinnamon buns, and Pavlova, a meringue creation decorated with kiwi and strawberries, made the choice difficult, so Anne decided to sample all of them.

The trilling of the phone brought Helen back into the present. She picked up the receiver. Bessie was calling from Padua. She had left on a bus trip to Italy with three of her friends and would miss today's festivities. They chatted for a few minutes. Bessie was enjoying the sights of Venice, Milan, and Florence while she checked out new recipes at Italian restaurants. Helen hung up and smiled. Her daughter, the cook. There had never been any doubt about Bessie's future, thanks to Rosa who had inspired Bessie's passion for cooking, and there was no better place to learn to become a gourmet chef than in Paris. She had enrolled in the French Culinary Institute in Paris, where she was in her last year. When she came home during vacations, she spent much of her time in the kitchen creating fabulous meals to everyone's delight, but there were still a few tricks to be learned from Rosa, and the two of them could often be found immersed in discussions about new culinary adventures.

Helen removed a beige linen dress from the closet and slipped it over her head. She walked over to the window. The profusion of color in the flower beds lining the front walk was breathtaking, and the lawn, which Fritz kept meticulously groomed, resembled a soft green carpet. She craned her head to look at the driveway. Fritz was removing smudges from the shiny, burgundy Mercedes with a soft cloth. She watched and smiled. The Mercedes was quite a change from the old DKW convertible, their first car after the war. She clearly remembered the day Fritz brought it home; its dents were too numerous to count, and they learned later that the roof collapsed during heavy rain. Quivering with excitement, the whole family had piled into the small vehicle. It sputtered and coughed, released a series of rapid blasts, and then took off in a cloud of smoke. They had traveled only three blocks on Ludwigstrasse, when the two rear tires released their last labored breath and the car descended slowly to the ground.

Helen kept watching as Fritz stepped back and proudly inspected the car. He raised his head quickly and caught her eye.

"Let's go. Rosa isn't going to be happy if we're late picking her up." Before she could answer, footsteps rang against the flagstone walk, and Anne skipped toward Fritz, her red hair fluttering in the breeze. She had grown quite tall and looked so pretty in her green jumper and white lace-trimmed blouse. Helen proudly gazed at father and daughter. They had developed a strong bond that belied all the resistance and hostility Anne had shown toward Fritz after he returned from the war.

Anne was the athlete in the family and delighted in the games and activities relegated to boys. Studying was not one of her passions, and it reflected in her grades, which improved drastically when she decided to join the student soccer team. The coach was reluctant to add a girl to the all boys' team, and Fritz met with him repeatedly to persuade him to take a chance on Anne. The coach finally agreed on one condition: she had to bring up her grades, which she did. When Anne joined the team, she became the subject of much harassment until she proved unequivocally that her skills matched those of any boy. She trained hard and held her own, setting a precedent that persuaded her friend Lilli to follow her lead. The current soccer team included four girls, and the school was proud of them.

In another year, Anne would be ready to go to the university. Fritz had insisted on allowing Anne to be her own person and transcend the limitations imposed by society upon young girls. He had assured Helen that, with maturity, the feminine side of Anne would make its appearance soon enough, and in time, her tomboy image slowly faded and she became interested in pretty clothes and fixing up her hair.

Helen stepped into a pair of black pumps. One last look in the mirror and she was reaching for her purse on the dressing table when her hand brushed against her grandson's photo, and she picked it up. Her eyes misted, and she looked at her parents' picture and whispered, "Look at him, Dad. Isn't he precious? How I wish you could be here and share this day with us."

Hermann stood tall in the picture; his wolf's head cane at his side. His eyes stared deeply into hers—those gentle gray eyes that would alternate between lighting up like fire when he was angry and exuding love and compassion when he comforted her. In a flash, he closed one eye and winked. It was as real as it could be, and Helen knew that Hermann would be with them today to join in his great-grandson's first birthday celebration. She blinked away her tears, blew him a kiss, and rushed out the door.

Karin Harrison left a successful career as an optician to return to college and concentrate on her writing. Her short stories have been published in books of anthology, literary journals and on line. *Hermann's Ruhe* is her first novel. Karin Harrison lives in Bel Air, Maryland.

23001994R00089

Made in the USA
Charleston, SC
10 October 2013